THE LIFE

VESPA

THE LIFE

VESPA

motorbooks

ERIC DREGNI

Brimming with creative inspiration, how-to projects, and useful information to enrich your everyday life, Quarto Knows is a favorite destination for those pursuing their interests and passions. Visit our site and dig deeper with our books into your area of interest: Quarto Creates, Quarto Cooks, Quarto Homes, Quarto Lives, Quarto Drives, Quarto Explores, Quarto Gifts, or Quarto Kids.

First published in 2018 by Motorbooks, an imprint of The Quarto Group, 401 Second Avenue North, Suite 310, Minneapolis, MN 55401 USA. T (612) 344-8100 F (612) 344-8692 www.QuartoKnows.com

Motorbooks titles are also available at discount for retail, wholesale, promotional, and bulk purchase. For details, contact the Special Sales Manager by email at specialsales@quarto.com or by mail at The Quarto Group, Attn: Special Sales Manager, 401 Second Avenue North, Suite 310, Minneapolis, MN 55401 USA.

10 9 8 7 6 5 4 3 2 1

ISBN: 978-0-7603-6043-9

Library of Congress Cataloging-in-Publication Data is on file.

Senior Editor: Darwin Holmstrom
Project Manager: Alyssa Lochner
Series Creative Director: Laura Drew
Page Design and Layout: Laura Drew and Beth Middleworth

On the front cover: Jean Seberg and Philippe Forquet in *In the French Style*. Photo courtesy Bettman/Getty Images. IN THE FRENCH STYLE © 1962, renewed 1990 Columbia Pictures Industries, Inc. All Rights Reserved. Courtesy of Columbia Pictures.

On the back cover: Johner Images/Alamy Stock Photo
On the endpapers: Trinity Mirror/Mirrorpix/Alamy Stock Photo
On the frontis: Shutterstock

Printed in China

CONTENTS

PREFACE

VESPA LOVE

THE PARTY HAD STARTED

Ska bands such as the Dig or the Funseekers shook the foundation of the huge parentless house, but what stole the show were two new Vespa P150s. I was just fifteen and I tried to dress to impress when I came here to the big city of St. Paul. I couldn't compete with those scooterists—dressed in hooded parkas, cuffed pants, and pointed black shoes—but it was the Vespas that the crowd of cute girls gathered around for a ride. I took the bus home, and knew I needed a scooter . . .

I peered through the storefront windows of the Vesparado store on University Avenue in hopes of picking up a scooter (and a girl) to bring to the next dance at the Prom Ballroom. The hefty price tag didn't fit the budget of a fifteen-year-old. Perhaps I could convince my parents to save the money that would send me to Italy as a foreign-exchange student the next year and instead "invest" these funds in a dangerous two-stroke scooter so I could give girls a ride around town. Somehow, they didn't buy it.

In Italy, scooters were everywhere— classic Vespas, Lambrettas, and myriad other sleek scooters that my Italian classmates posed on in the piazza, passing the evening chatting and smoking cigarettes with an occasional two-person ride up to the castle on the hill. Vincenzio gave me a ride on the back of his Vespa P150. He twisted the throttle and let out the clutch, and away we roared. He zipped down the cobblestones, and the roar of the muffler echoed off the walls and down the tunnel-like roads. He swerved uphill on a street with low 2-inch steps and the shock absorbers stuttered with each bump. I was terrified by this exhilarating ride from a fellow teenager with an apparent death wish. He screeched the scooter to a stop at the top of the hill near the castle, with the lights of distant hill towns flicking across the valley. "See?" he said. "A Vespa can take you anywhere." Then he blasted the gas and didn't coast down the hill, but accelerated as if brakes were for sissies. To stop, he burned rubber in the front of everyone. We'd been gone just three minutes, but I now knew why every Italian teenager must have a Vespa. Why was I denied these two-wheeled wings under my feet?

When I returned to the US, I was determined to find my own wheels.

My friend TJ bought a classic Lambretta TV150 in a St. Paul suburb from a man named Vern who had grown far too wide for his scooter to haul him to the strip mall. Vern had "upgraded" to a giant 1,000cc Honda motorcycle and scoffed at his old scooter. "If you want speed, get a Goldwing!" he said as he patted his belly. He didn't understand that it's not about actual speed but about the illusion of speed. If you're zooming through the piazza at 60 miles per hour, who can see you?

I knew more of these scooters had to be around since Sears had imported Vespas and rebranded them as Allstates and Montgomery Ward brought in Lambrettas. Piaggio had ceased selling scooters in the US, allegedly out of concern about American product-liability laws, but more likely because of slumped sales. Aren't scooters supposed to be somewhat dangerous?

Because of this dearth of cool new Italian scooters, prices soared for used ones. A man in Minneapolis wanted to sell me his ratty old white Vespa for $600, a small fortune at the time. I examined everything I'd have to fix, and his sales pitch was, "Look at all the things that still work!"

I'd heard of an entrepreneur in Chicago who went to Italy and bought up old Vespas and sent them to the US in a giant shipping container to jack up the prices for eager teenagers like me. I'd even heard that some young wannabe scooterists scoured auctions in small towns looking for old Vespas that farmers picked up from Sears on a whim. My friend Willy found the pinnacle of Piaggio's designs, a Vespa GS, and talked about "saving its soul" by restoring it to pristine condition.

Instead, my brother Michael and I found two classic scooters for less than $200 for the pair and spent the next year trying to find parts to fix them up. It was then that we also found a 1957 Vespa in Illinois. I couldn't afford to fix up two scooters, so my friend Steve bought the Vespa and, with Willy, spent more than a year restoring it to perfect condition. They put the finishing touches on it and left it in Willy's barn to be driven the next morning. That night, the barn burned down. Teary-eyed, they showed me photos of the precious Vespa in flames.

My brother and I set up our scooter-repair shop in his dark basement and nicknamed it Breath of Exhaust Scooter De-Tuning Works. Wouldn't women flock to a guy sleeping in a basement covered in grease and surrounded by paint fumes? I was betting on it.

I had just finished a mod two-tone paint scheme, but my lack of mechanical skills led me to stripping nuts and bolts and otherwise making my scooter a less than reliable ride. I knew the trick, from having lived in Italy, that you tell your girlfriend that the engine just conked out in some remote, romantic locale. Explaining to my date that it really did break down and we had to push it back did not lead to a second date. I started a mock support group for bad mechanics, Bolt-strippers Anonymous, with the motto "Ne'er too tight is a bolt."

Over time, I bored out my scooter's engine for more horsepower and filled the tank with jet fuel for added speed. I reached 60 miles per hour down a big hill in Wisconsin on those little 10-inch wheels—and scared myself straight. Most important, I changed out the single saddle for a long bench seat so a potential date could hold on tight. It took a decade, but my scheme did work; I found the right girl. The first time we met, I gave her a lift home on the bench seat. I knew it: scooters equal love.

CHAPTER
ONE

DAWN OF THE SCOOTER

POST OFFICE
EMPLOYEES ENTRANCE NO ADMISSION
EMPLOYEES ENTRANCE NO ADMISSION

WHAT IS A "SCOOTER"?

Leonardo da Vinci drew a design for the first bicycle—or was it a scooter? The Italian language makes a clear distinction between a motorized scooter and a child's scooter (a monopattino) or single roller skate. Still, the motor scooter borrows the crucial floorboards and small wheels. Most of all, scooters are a fun and quick way to bop around town. The earliest scooter made in large numbers was the American Autoped, "Wonder of the Motor Vehicle World," looking less like a step-through motorcycle than a motorized child's toy. UK Imperial Motor Industries built an Autoped with minor improvements to the original, and in 1919 Townsend Engineering Co. of Birmingham created the Autoglider De Luxe, which claimed a top speed of 50km/h. Bold scooterists claimed to have reached 80km/h, although probably on a steep slope.

Also in 1919, the British made the ABC Skootamota and a French ad pushed the scooter as the perfect means to move down the Champs-Elysées:

"If Madame has to meet a friend at 11 o'clock at the Bois de Boulogne, at noon be at home for lunch, then shop at the big stores downtown, and later in the evening dine with friends in the suburbs, she would never be able to do all this by taking outrageously priced taxis that are impossible to flag down. Knowing this, Madame bought a SKOOTAMOTA, the woman's machine 'par excellence' which is easy to drive, doesn't demand any mechanical knowledge, and doesn't need a garage."

The French, however, claim an even earlier scooter, the 1902 Auto-Fauteuil, but the Danes have unearthed one from before that. Even Gottlieb Daimler's first motorcycle from 1885 had distinct scooter-like qualities. Piaggio eventually perfected the scooter's design with the Vespa, produced in Pisa not far from the town of Vinci. Perhaps we could trace this all back to da Vinci after all.

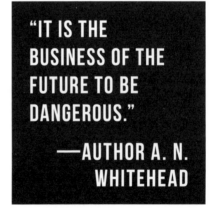

"IT IS THE BUSINESS OF THE FUTURE TO BE DANGEROUS."

—AUTHOR A. N. WHITEHEAD

THE PAPERINO
DONALD DUCK'S SCOOTER

Benito Mussolini extolled the virtues of all things Italian and bristled at foreign infiltration into his new Roman Empire. Still, his kids liked Mickey Mouse and Donald Duck, whose names were conveniently changed to Topolino (little mouse) and Paperino (gosling) to avoid Italian censors and Disney's copyright lawyers. Mussolini famously ripped off his shirt to show his bulging muscles on top of a FIAT tractor. FIAT as well had a soft spot for Walt Disney characters and named its people's car the Topolino in honor of the little American mouse. Mussolini even hosted Walt Disney himself in 1935 at Palazzo Venezia in Rome, where Mussolini would give his famous speeches from the balcony to fired-up crowds of fascists. Walt gave Il Duce a giant wooden Mickey for his kids. Despite FIAT's and Mussolini's love for Mickey, the humorless fascist censors cut off Italian publication of Disney comics in 1942.

Meanwhile, scooter prototypes sprung up in Italy that clearly copied many of the American scooters already on the roads, in particular the Cushman Autoglide. In 1938, FIAT made essentially the first Italian scooter but never put it into production. FIAT's scooting ambitions were eclipsed by the war, but SIMAT succeeded in building one of the first Italian scooters in 1940. Across town in Turin, Aermoto built the little Volugrafo parachuting scooter to help the fascists annex Albania and conquer King Zog without a single shot fired.

With heavy Allied bombing of Italian factories, Piaggio moved out of Tuscany to the city of Biella in Piedmont—not far from FIAT's headquarters in Turin. Enrico Piaggio was so impressed by the Aermoto that he put designers Vittorio Casini and Renzo Spolti to work on a scooter based on the SIMAT. Perhaps Piaggio was trying to make amends to Il Duce for accidentally killing Mussolini's son when a Piaggio P.108B plane crashed.

Piaggio's engineers took many of the styling cues from FIAT, SIMAT, and Volugrafo prototypes to make the precursor of the Vespa. They added a leg shield and nicknamed their 1944 creation the Paperino, or Donald Duck, probably a poke in the eye to the Italian censors, who still prohibited those dangerous Disney comics that threatened to defeat fascism. When the war ended, Piaggio got the go-ahead from the Allies to build the Paperino. Estimates of actual production numbers of the handmade Duck range from ten to one hundred, and only two are known to still exist. In the end, the gravelly voiced gosling won the war. Piaggio's designer Corradino D'Ascanio would later mold the duck into a wasp, the Vespa.

THE DEBUT OF THE VESPA:
EXCESS IN THE AGE OF AUSTERITY

After World War II, Italy was in shambles, and people scrimped and saved just to have enough bread and wine to survive. Imagine Vespa's audacious debut at the 1946 Turin show. Corradino D'Ascanio designed a thoroughly modern automobile with luscious curves and excessive use of metal to cover the engine—all in an age of austerity. Most motorcycling aficionados scoffed at this diminutive little toy and would rather double their horsepower and ride on larger wheels for greater distances. Obviously they didn't understand Piaggio's dream.

Sure, the original Vespa had flaws, but the quirks would soon be worked out. The suspension was "soft," causing dangerous dips at sudden stops. The puny 8-inch wheels would sink into potholes, causing the scooter to lose control or perhaps fling the rider over the handlebars. The right-mounted engine made the whole scooter lean (especially if the left-mounted spare tire was removed as ballast). And the sparking was unreliable at best.

Fortunately, the war-torn public understood D'Ascanio's vision and recognized something beautiful in an age when many buildings were rubble: an intrepid new form of transport with style. Nearby in Milan, Piaggio's biggest rival, Innocenti, quietly took notes at the 1946 Turin show and succeeded in avoiding the Vespa's flaws in its forthcoming Lambretta scooter. The early Lambrettas caved to motorcyclists, however, who didn't want all the unnecessary (but cool) metal covering over the engine, floorboard, wheels, and handlebars. A new age had dawned in which the public didn't want to see the huffing-puffing dirty engines, yet they still wanted speed and splendor.

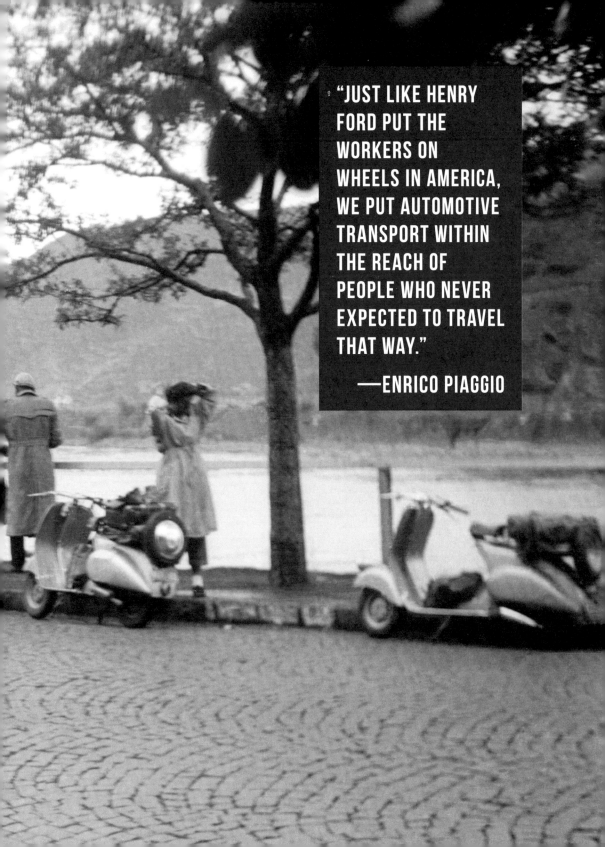

"JUST LIKE HENRY FORD PUT THE WORKERS ON WHEELS IN AMERICA, WE PUT AUTOMOTIVE TRANSPORT WITHIN THE REACH OF PEOPLE WHO NEVER EXPECTED TO TRAVEL THAT WAY."

—ENRICO PIAGGIO

FLATTENED FACTORIES . . . AND OTHER SCOOTER-MAKING SETBACKS

Because Piaggio made military planes during World War II, the factory was a favorite target for Allied bombing raids. Postwar, Piaggio was prohibited from making war-related materiel. A probably apocryphal legend states that designer Corradino D'Ascanio found some old airplane wheels and forks in the wreckage of the Piaggio factory and pieced together the first Vespa. The wasp scooter was the phoenix rising from the ashes of World War II.

Before the war, factories became the symbol of technological progress for Constructivists—and any other politician, for that matter. Smokestacks puffing out soot meant jobs, and Italians took pride in being indeed part of the industrialized world.

Enrico Piaggio looked to Ford's assembly lines and surrounding worker communities to turn factories into a symbol of pride. In 1956, he told *Time* magazine, "Just like Henry Ford put the workers on wheels in America, we put automotive transport within the reach of people who never expected to travel that way."

Piaggio turned the small town of Pontedera near Pisa into a working community, and citizens came from all over Italy looking for jobs. Piaggio and Innocenti, the latter of which made the Lambretta, set up "factory communities" with swimming pools and tennis courts to keep the workers happy. These factories become a mecca of progress in the dark days after the war. The Vespa was cheap enough that these families could afford their very first "car on two wheels."

Through technology and science, the symbol of perfection had risen to conquer the world: the production line. Piaggio produced a promotional film about its factory that won the prize for best nonfiction film at the Cannes Film Festival of 1961. The Piaggio factory became a model for making Vespas abroad in Belgium, Brazil, France, Spain, Germany, India, and England. From humble beginnings in an old sawmill in 1884 to making the first air-cooled engines for airplanes, Piaggio could boast that it put the world on two wheels.

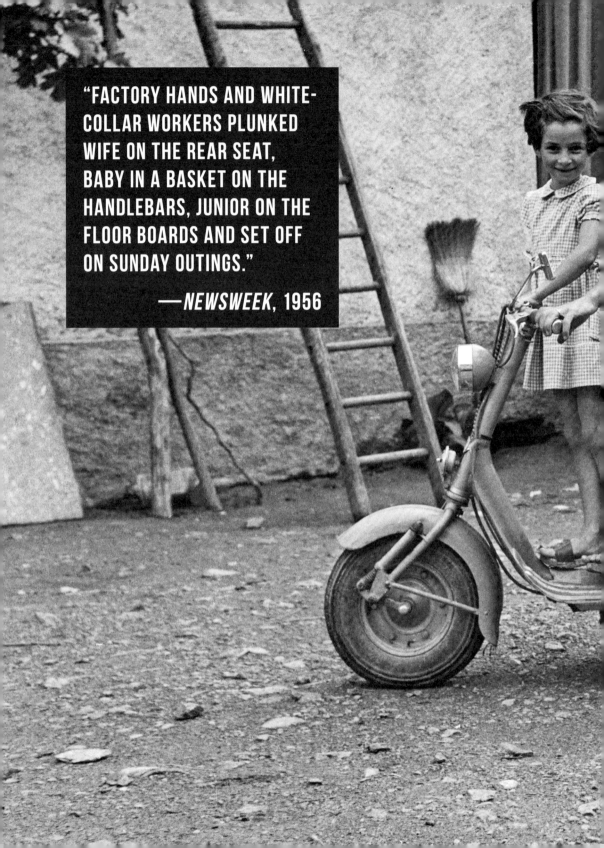

"FACTORY HANDS AND WHITE-COLLAR WORKERS PLUNKED WIFE ON THE REAR SEAT, BABY IN A BASKET ON THE HANDLEBARS, JUNIOR ON THE FLOOR BOARDS AND SET OFF ON SUNDAY OUTINGS."

—*NEWSWEEK*, 1956

THE POLITICS OF THE VESPA

After Mussolini was unceremoniously strung up on a gas-station light post in Milan's Piazza Loreto, partisans looked to see who else collaborated with the fascists. Most industrialists played both sides, since they were businessmen. Enrico Piaggio described those immediate postwar days to *American Mercury* magazine in 1957: "Our over ten thousand employees were thrown out of work by the bombings and by the fact that, as soon as the war was over, our production fell to zero. In fact, we were prohibited from making airplanes by the peace treaty. So you see it was essential that we find a new peacetime product for the sake of the Piaggio company and our employees." Thus the Vespa.

The remaining fascists went into hiding in the 1950s and '60s, so the Italian Communist Party became the majority party, even if the CIA made sure it never came to power. Enrico Piaggio deemed it his patriotic duty to put his Vespa within reach of Italians to lure them away from Marx. In 1952, he told *Time* magazine, "The best way to fight Communism in this country is to give each worker a scooter, so he will have his own transportation,

have something valuable of his own, and have a stake in the principle of private property." Suddenly, the super-cool Vespa became a political tool to expand capitalism in Italy.

Reader's Digest exalted Enrico Piaggio as "the man who put Italy on two wheels," but not all his workers had such kind thoughts. In those poverty-stricken postwar years, they desperately needed the jobs, and Piaggio took advantage of the staggering unemployment to keep wages painfully low. Still, workers flocked to Pontedera in search of any job, even if it meant giving up some freedom to the company store.

Some employees bristled at the official Piaggio "propaganda" in the company magazine that promoted the "resounding workshops of Pontedera" where "the commitment of every single worker to production perfection is honed and strengthened by spontaneous desire and enlightened passion." *La Nazione* newspaper in nearby Florence bought the marketing blitz and hailed Pontedera as a "happy Tuscan town" because of the Piaggio factory. The journalist then received nasty notes from the workers and

their union showing how pitifully low their wages were.

During labor strikes, Piaggio hauled in nonunion workers in trucks to pass the picket lines of protesting union workers. The company gave plum positions to workers who were part of the center-right Christian Democrats and turned down promotions to members of the trade union CGIL, The Confederazione Generale Italiana del Lavoro. The union struck back by revealing salaries of the bosses and the alleged profit pocketed by each Vespa sold. Piaggio hired special company police to conduct spot searches for left-wing political literature—they even removed restroom stall doors when workers were caught passing pamphlets in the bathroom—and follow workers outside the plant to monitor whether they joined unions.

Piaggio survived the controversies, and conditions eventually improved for all involved. The company invested heavily in building affordable housing for its workers and built the "Piaggio Village" with a library, a hotel, a sports facilities, a community center, and a church. Perhaps to smooth over past confrontations, Piaggio even had an official vacation colony along the Italian Riviera in Liguria at the tiny town of Santo Stefano d'Aveto, but most likely managers got first dibs.

"THE BEST WAY TO FIGHT COMMUNISM IN THIS COUNTRY IS TO GIVE EACH WORKER A SCOOTER."

—ENRICO PIAGGIO

CHAPTER TWO

THE VESPA AESTHETIC

FASTER! LOUDER!
MAKING A "BELLA FIGURA" ON A VESPA

Vespas are cool. Anyone who disagrees obviously doesn't have one and has never ridden one. The Italian concept of making a "bella figura," or making a good impression, is intrinsically linked to the Vespa, and the only way to make a scooter better is to saw off the exhaust pipe to make the motor zoom even faster—and louder. This 10 percent power increase is much easier than investing oodles of time and cash into boring out the engine for added velocity, and the new oomph is essential for cruising the piazza. The result is even better gas mileage to this two-wheeled Italian hot rod, but also an illegal decibel increase—look out for the fuzz!

THE VESPA 150 HAS A "HORN LIKE A MODEL T'S WITH A FOREIGN ACCENT."

—POPULAR SCIENCE, 1957

Not everyone is convinced. A journalist from *Fortune* magazine visited Europe in 1956 and denigrated Italians and their scooters in one fell swoop: "In Italy, where people are a lot less well-heeled than in America . . . many Vespa owners feel that a little extra mileage is well worth a lot of extra noise." The author bemoaned, "Not content with making the Italian night hideous, Piaggio & Co. of Genoa, which manufactures one of Italy's most popular scooters, the Vespa, has launched a determined assault on the American market." Soon, the US would be victim to the Vespa engine's "sound of riveting guns."

The Italian invasion had arrived in 1956, and *Business Week* wrote condescendingly of "Italians' Latin enthusiasm" with "their little machines." Even the erudite *New Yorker* warned of the impending assault of Vespas blasting down Broadway: "Motor scooters, the current scourge of sleep in Italian cities, have established a beachhead here." Partially, the American press worried that the much more

La Bonne Vie!

Discover the exhilaration of a Vespa ride . . . a r
kind of life that takes you places. You'll love
freedom of Vespa, take pride in its flawless cra
manship and performance. Vespa is styled for
young at heart.

A symphony of incomparable beauty and riding pl
sure . . . soft as Italian silk . . . heady as Rivi
wine . . . keyed to the style of the future with
quiet power. Designed and engineered by craftsr
of quality.

Sold and serviced in the United States by franchi
Cushman dealers.

For free literature or dealer name, contact:

CUSHMAN MOTORS 1077 No. 21 St. LINCOLN, N

A subsidiary of Outboard Marine Corporation

CUSHMAN Vespa

elegant and reliable Vespa would put the homespun Cushman scooters out of business.

The usually restrained *National Geographic* also couldn't refrain from belittling the fantastically popular Vespa in a 1957 feature on Italy: "Roaring, darting scooters, outnumbering automobiles, dominate Rome's traffic. These toylike vehicles have swept Italy since the war, almost replacing the motorcycle."

Popular Science magazine tested a Vespa 150 in 1957 and gave an unbiased report, even if the writer couldn't resist some quips. The motor sounded like a "vacuum cleaner" with "a polite but busy whisper," and the "horn like a Model T's with a foreign accent." The journalist admitted that the "Vespa claims the lowest decibel noise count of any scooter." Of course, that's easily cured with a hacksaw to the tailpipe. Remember that speed equals noise, thanks to the lack of a muffler.

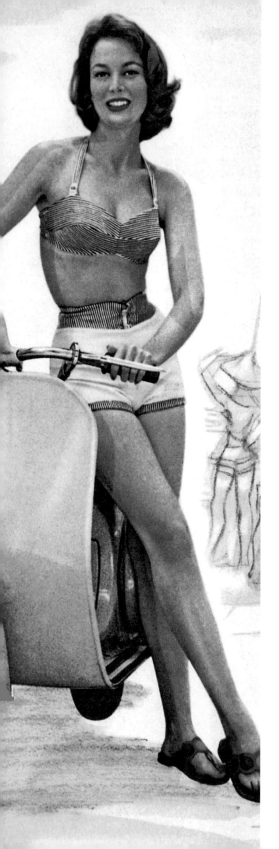

THE SCOOTER'S SIX COMMANDMENTS

The inventor of the Vespa, Corradino D'Ascanio, was more than a designer; he was a sort of scooter philosopher. He espoused six basic principles that all (successful) scooters must follow. Some brands fiddled with D'Ascanio's rules, but they inevitably were left by the wayside:

1. The scooter must be easy to drive.

2. Weight must be kept to a minimum.

3. Just like a woman's bicycle is easy to mount, so must a scooter be.

4. The gearshift shall be mounted on the handlebars for easy handling.

5. The driver must be kept clean by the front leg shield, floor panels, and covered engine.

6. A spare tire must be incorporaed into the design of the scooter and shall be easy to change.

THE THEORY OF SPEED
RELATIVITY BE DAMNED!

Speed is relative, and time is shaped by relativity—just ask Einstein. Feeling speed isn't the same as traveling quickly. We are spinning 24,000 miles a day around the earth's axis and flying around the sun each year, but we don't even muss up our hair on the way. Not so on a Vespa. Twist the throttle and feel the terror of dodging distracted car drivers talking on their cell phones, smoking cigarettes, and putting on makeup. Sure, a Ferrari Testa Rossa can zip away at 200 miles per hour, but the thrill of a riding atop a Vespa's mini wheels, nearly vertical front fork, and buzzing two-stroke engine tempts the Grim Reaper and brings the rider one step closer to the scooter netherworld. This is speed.

The Italian futurists knew that "the world's magnificence has been enriched by a new beauty; the beauty of speed." F. T. Marinetti declared a "Religion of Speed" that worshipped the "aesthetics of the machine." In other words, speedsters needed to go fast and look good. Otherwise, what's the point? Marinetti was the ultimate modernist, declaring that "we want no part of the past" and "time and space died yesterday." Suddenly with these new machines, such as the Vespa, no one was restricted to their little town but could go anywhere—and fast.

French cultural theorist Jean Baudrillard agreed that speed was the new aesthetic: "Speed creates pure objects. It is itself a pure object, since it cancels out the ground and territorial reference-points, since it runs ahead of time to annul time itself . . ." Perhaps most people viewed the Vespa as a simple means of transportation, but once scooterists got the bug for speed, who would return to walking?

"ROARING, DARTING SCOOTERS, OUTNUMBERING AUTOMOBILES, DOMINATE ROME'S TRAFFIC."

—*NATIONAL GEOGRAPHIC*, 1957

SAFETY LAST
THE FUTURE IS NOW AND DANGEROUS

> "TO TURN A FOURTEEN-YEAR-OLD CHILD LOOSE ON A MOTOR SCOOTER IN TODAY'S TRAFFIC IS ABOUT AS SENSIBLE AS GIVING A BABY A DYNAMITE CAP FOR A TEETHING RING."
>
> —GEN. GEORGE C. STEWART, NATIONAL SAFETY COUNCIL, 1956

The Vespa age riled pessimists to declare that the scooter's supposed instability would cause drivers to crash in a fiery mess, unaware that the bane of any scooterist's existence is actually the automobile. *Atlantic Monthly* warned in 1962 that "scooters are inherently unstable, like spinning tops. . . . On a scooter you lean over, and there you are, upside down in the ditch. You have to influence the scooter around a corner in a series of more or less controlled wobbles."

General George C. Stewart of the National Safety Council declared, "I would rather have a fourteen-year-old child of mine turned loose in traffic with a ten-ton truck than on a scooter." Yes, but what about the pedestrians that the child runs down in the truck?

The dangers for even the boldest *vespisti* are fierce. *Popular Science* uncovered some of the pitfalls for Vespa riders in a 1957 article, warning, "Dogs are conservative animals easily outraged by the unconventional and will frisk alongside munching at your heels." Never mind that the leg shields protect the scooterist, unlike motorcyclists, who have nothing to keep Fido at bay. At the same time, the article encouraged scooter folly: "Snow, however, is navigable if you know your stuff." Scooter shortcomings were conveniently overlooked, as seen in forgiving text like, "You can see behind simply by turning your head." The mods fixed that problem by adding a dozen mirrors.

The *New York Times* magazine also downplayed the danger in a 1958 article, declaring with questionable

logic, "These machines have a low center of gravity and if they fall over you're right there on the ground. Safer than if an accident happens in a closed car."

Piaggio clearly avoided talking of the danger on two wheels. Aftermarket pillion seats even featured a sidesaddle version, which of course makes the center of gravity even more precarious.

Out of necessity, whole families hopped on to the family scooter, despite the danger. "Women ride, too. When papa drives, mamma sits sidesaddle on the box seat, often with a baby in her lap," wrote *National Geographic* in 1957. "Youngsters stand between seat and handlebars." Imagine the fun of tipping the Vespa at 35 miles per hour with five passengers! Scooterists remembered the words of historian A. N. Whitehead, who knew that "it is the business of the future to be dangerous."

WHY THE VESPA IS "MODERN"
DOWN WITH MOTORCYCLES!

> **"THE WHEEL IS AN EXTENSION OF THE FOOT."**
>
> **—CULTURAL THEORIST MARSHALL McLUHAN ESPOUSING HUMANKIND'S NATURAL EVOLUTION TO RIDING A VESPA**

In 1945, Europeans saw the past as a disaster. With flattened cities and unplanted fields of mud, Europe after World War II was decimated, and the culprits who allowed this carnage were ugly tanks, bombers, and motorcycles. Mechanical violence propelled the Industrial Revolution to unprecedented destruction. Smoke-spewing factories destroyed all visions of paradise and represented imminent aggression. No longer was the engine beautiful.

The Italian futurists, such as Marinetti, had preached that "war is the world's only hygiene," but two world wars brought only destruction and misery. The motorcycle was the two-wheeled steed of war and the ultimate expression of masculinity. Now the world wanted rebirth and longed for the beauty of the feminine. Just as a ship is always a "she," so was the Vespa dreamed up as a woman with curvaceous lines hiding a purring motor beneath its hip-like side panels. After all, "vespa" is a feminine noun in Italian.

The scooter visionary Corradino D'Ascanio recognized this new modernity and the need for designed appliances that were both aesthetically pleasing and highly functional. As a modern Renaissance man, D'Ascanio could finally incorporate his engineering and technological skill with artistic panache, much as Brunelleschi had done centuries before with Florence's cathedral. Italian designers such as Ghia, Pininfarina, Pierluigi Torre, and D'Ascanio could focus on making the immediate needs of Italian families beautiful—from Bialetti espresso makers to the Cisitalia Coupe, from sculpturally interesting and comfortable chairs to the nearly perfect Vespa GS. Finally the war was over, and the brilliance of

two millennia of Italian creativity could be reignited to make a modern means of mobility for a new era. The brilliant Italian design struck a chord with many middle- and lower-class British and Italian youth who rejected their parents' industrial work ethic, which only got them another faceless row house and grueling factory job.

Owning a Vespa, which most anyone could afford, represented freedom and a new world of harmony and innovation in a classless society. The dirty, macho motorcycle may carry the rider away from civilization and the maddening city; the scooter brings people together in the city as the ultimate urban—and modern—vehicle.

VESPA'S PERFECT DESIGN
"SO GOOD LOOKING IT MUST BE ITALIAN!"

The sleek lines of the Vespa have become unmistakable, and its name has become synonymous with "scooter" in many languages. No wonder *Design* magazine proclaimed in 1949 that "the most important of all new Italian design phenomena is without doubt the Vespa" at the forefront of the "Second Italian Renaissance." Roll over, Michelangelo! To echo this praise, the Guggenheim Museum in New York prominently featured the Vespa GS in 1996 as the crowned jewel of modern Italian design.

The design fulfilled all the necessities called for in a scooter; however, Corradino D'Ascanio went beyond just function to make the form of the Vespa truly beautiful. Rising from the wreckage of a bombed factory, Piaggio's postwar saga began when he made a few sketches in February 1945 of a prototype scooter called MP6, with a unique monocoque body that essentially attached the leg shields and covering to the frame. His experience designing helicopters and other such vehicles allowed him to iron out any flaws to improve the Vespa and mobilize the masses across Italy and eventually the world.

The Vespa became the dream machine of teenagers, who instantly recognized the beauty not only of speed but of design. In 1956, *Mechanix Illustrated* praised Vespa's sleek shape as "So good looking that it must be Italian!" The ugliness of the war from the previous decade was forgotten. Giovanni Agnelli, who later

> "SCOOTERS EVADE BARRIERS, JUMP OVER TRAFFIC ISLANDS, CUT THROUGH PARKS, BUMP DOWN HILLS OR STEPS, AND SLICE THROUGH NARROW OPENINGS."
>
> —THE *AMERICAN CITY MAGAZINE,* 1966

became owner of FIAT and Piaggio, proclaimed, "I'm profoundly convinced that the history and successes of Piaggio—along with its failures and less happy times—are intimately tied to Italian exuberance that is part of our genetic makeup." He essentially charted a direct line from da Vinci to modern Italian designers such as D'Ascanio.

The snooty *Atlantic Monthly* wasn't quite so kind and declared in 1962 that "the makers of Vespas . . . use economy and maneuverability as their two main selling points. For many people, these are enough to make up for their relative lack of comfort." The writer

missed entirely Vespa's classic design. Never mind, because the Vespa was a smash. "By 1956, 1.5 million scooters were on the roads in Italy," according to *Newsweek*, and most were Vespas. Today, more than 16 million Vespas—a staggering number—have been made.

SCOOTER CLUBS OF
THE WORLD UNITE!

SCOOTER CLUBS
PUTT-PUTT GANGS GO WILD

Anyone who has ever driven one knows a Vespa is far more than just a means of transportation. Comedian Jay Leno, who usually drives fancy automobiles and powerful motorcycles, described riding a Vespa: "Women come up and go, 'What's that?' You explain it, then you have to explain that you're married."

Romance blossoms on a Vespa as scooterists search for someone to ride with them. A 1957 *Popular Science* article described this amorous vehicle: "Sports riders in this country are mostly either single or newly marrieds (scooters are so conducive to romance that there is a fast turnover between these categories)."

While cars shield drivers from the outside world, Vespas open riders up to meet new people. Scooterists buzz through piazzas and meet at cafés. "This is more than a fad, it's a revolution, and I don't see how anything can stop it," the *New Yorker* warned in 1957. Italy especially was irrevocably changed for the better.

To put order to this new social order, Adolf Nass formed the first Vespa Club in 1951 in Saarbrücken, Germany. Because the scooter is a social appliance, Vespa riders were already meeting, but now the clubs made these groups official. More than three hundred clubs sprouted up around the globe, as well as 1,200 Vespa service stations.

Most clubs went on rides or socialized on weekends, but some set down strict protocol: "It's an unwritten code for scooterists to greet each other," said a Vespa rider in the *New York Times Magazine* in 1958. In the era before cell phones, Vespa etiquette expected a rider to lend a hand to a fellow vespista broken down on the side of the road, even if the driver had never even looked under the side panels before.

"As you well know," announced Renato Tassinari at the 10th Annual Congress of the Vespa Club d'Italia, "we are a movement based exclusively on goodness, with none of the poison of political hatred, none of the rigidity of hazy or unreachable idealism; a movement that comes about, expresses itself, and breeds to the beat of small engines and hearts serene." Compare this sunny disposition to the dismal reputation of Hells Angels or other motorcycle gangs.

Motorcycle movies inevitably had the cliché long-distance trips that often terrorized a small town, but scooters thrived in the city. Author Bill Buford proclaimed that "the Vespa is the world's greatest urban vehicle. . . . Its natural home is the city. New York, like Rome, needs to be lived on foot to appreciate its infinite mystery—not by subway or taxi car. But you'll see more of its mystery if you can be motored around it in the open air."

Even the macho *Motociclismo* magazine gave a hesitant nod to Vespas in 1946 as perhaps a better vehicle for everyone. "It is a vehicle which, unlike the traditional motorcycle proper, is suitable for all social classes and for both sexes. . . . It is the ideal vehicle for short trips to town for businessmen, professionals, doctors, etc."

Piaggio envisioned its Vespa uniting the country, not to be used as a rebel's ride for the "Wild One." Italy during the 1950s and '60s was rocked with political turmoil that threatened the government. The majority Italian Communist Party could have ruled the country, except it was kept out of power by the CIA—and the Vespa. Enrico Piaggio decided it was his patriotic duty make his scooter available to the workers to lure them away from communism.

Word spread partially through scooter newsletters, such as *Vespa News, Lambretta Leader,* and *Jet-Set,* which were translated into numerous languages for the loyal scooter legions. Sometimes, though, these Vespa clubs almost seemed too prim and proper. A Vespa club profiled in a 1956 *New Yorker* article asked rhetorically, "What are the club's purposes?" and answered: "Thinking up scooter trips, getting discounts on spare parts, lobbying for the abolition of such laws as the one that keeps us off parkways." The next year, the *New Yorker* ran another piece glorifying Vespas as the solution to the Big Apple's traffic and the police's alleged permissiveness to scooter riders: "Truth is, nobody seems to mind what scooters do. They're a kind of delightful toy that happens to do a car-size job."

Not everyone was so charmed. In 1966, the *American City Magazine* complained about these supposedly lawless vespisti: "Scooters evade barriers, jump over traffic islands, cut through parks, bump down hills or steps, and slice through narrow openings."

The debate raged about whether Vespas were a large vehicle like a car or motorcycle, which must follow the rules of the road, or more similar to a bicycle or even a pedestrian that could make use of the sidewalks. The *New York Times Magazine* backed up Vespa riders in 1957, claiming that "scooterists emphasize that they drive for pleasure, not for speed." Also in 1957 the *New Yorker* defended the straight-laced scooterists as "an increasing number of quietly dressed, sober-looking scooterists of both sexes and a variety of ages darting amiably, by day and night, through the thick of midtown traffic."

Vespa clubs knew that they must uphold their reputation, since abolishing the Vespa from city life would fling society back into the past. Cultural theorist Dick Hebdige declared that "the scooter serves as the material bridge between different generations, different cultures, different epochs, between contradictory desires. It is a sign of progress. . . . It is a passport to the future." The clubs brought young and old scooter riders together to ride vintage Vespas or the latest models far and wide.

SIDE-SADDLE NO MORE!
"UNTAMED, UNMANICURED . . . BITTER ITALIAN BEAUTIES"

Scooters were designed with women in mind. *Popular Mechanics* wrote in 1947, "As the family's second 'car,' the scooter makes shopping a pleasure for the housewife." Originally a tool to help keep a housewife chained to her suburban kitchen, scooters helped emancipate women when Amelia Earhart was pictured on top of an American Motoped scooter. Before the Vespa hit the scene, suffragists in the early 1900s zipped around American and British cities on Autopeds and ABC Skootamotas. Sure, suburban husbands wanted their darling wives to shop for that prime rib for supper, but women found newfound freedom on two wheels.

Just as designers fashioned these early stand-up scooters for women, so did Piaggio when Corradino D'Ascanio envisioned *donne* in dresses as his main market. With Italian women on his mind, he made lusciously curvaceous side panels covering the engine to avoid grease splatter and a protruding front shield to keep rain and sand from splattering the latest Milanese fashions. Many gussied-up Italian women insisted on high heels, so the motorcycle's footgear shifter was replaced by a left-sided, twisting handle to drop the wasp into a higher gear. The step-through frame, with no ugly gas tank between the rider's legs, allowed for proper dresses to dangle elegantly with the front leg shield protecting from any unwanted Marilyn Monroe updrafts. The *New York Times Magazine* concurred in 1958 that the Vespa's design made for more attractive women: "Another visible difference is that scooters do not have a center bar for the driver to straddle. This makes for more girl riders and less Ghent-to-Aix forward lean."

Despite the obvious issues of men envisioning attractive women driving scooters, many magazines still relegated women to the back seat: the pillion. "Two persons can ride one at the same time, but a woman wearing a skirt (particularly if it is a straight one) must ride sidesaddle if she is the passenger," wrote *Popular Mechanics* in 1957. Piaggio supposedly remedied this dangerous position in 1957, when a Vespa accessory catalog featured a Poltrovespa sidesaddle seat with a backrest. That same year, a *National*

Geographic feature on Italy showed a woman on a scooter, but it put her in the back seat.

Even male British mods, according to Dick Hebdige, sometimes belittled their girls as mere "pillion fodder." In the US, attitudes in the monthly *American Mercury* in 1957 weren't much better: "Young couples, she riding sidesaddle prettily and revealingly and he, heading deliberately for every bump to jounce her into holding him tighter."

Fortunately, female Vespa riders didn't buy this garbage. Unabashed Italian divas like Gina Lollobrigida and Anna Magnani zoomed around on Vespas and blew exhaust in the faces of those gawking men. In 1954, *Picture Post* wrote about this "New Race of Girls" as "untamed, unmanicured, proud, passionate, bitter Italian beauties [on their] clean, sporting Vespa."

Piaggio was proud to put women in the driver's seat, since it recognized the new market. The admen couldn't resist, and exploited this image in cheesecake calendar photos, but at least the suggestively clad beauties were in control of the scooter rather than splayed across the car or motorcycle as eye candy. In the 1954 advertising film *Travel Far, Travel Wide*, the scooter is the centerpiece of the battle of the sexes. A stylish stewardess descends the ramp from the plane to the tarmac and hops on her scooter. A narrator proclaims, "The air hostess can become the pilot herself—and there's plenty of room on that pillion for a friend!" The man hops on the back seat; the woman finally takes control.

> "I DISCOVERED THAT THE SCOOTER PROVIDED A RELIABLE LITMUS TEST OF MALE CHARACTER."
> —*MS.* MAGAZINE, 1987

FEMALE VESPA CLUBS
OUTRIDING, OUTRACING THE MEN

After the scooter slump of the 1970s, women rediscovered the vehicle that was made with them in mind. With the twilight of the mod revolution, female vespisti were fed up with being referred to as "pillion fodder," so they hopped off the back seat and took over the handlebars. By the mid-1980s, the feminist press finally embraced the scooter as its ride. "I discovered that the scooter provided a reliable litmus test of male character," wrote Letty Cottin Pogrebin in *Ms.* magazine in 1987. "Those who were threatened by it didn't last long in my affections."

Woman's Day also featured a piece that same year about the thrill and freedom of driving a Vespa and equated it to a businessman putting on leather and chaps to ride a Harley on the weekend: "I'd never made a serious move about getting a scooter. I knew as well as anyone that cars come swinging around curves and there you are, tossed in the air like a matador on the horns of a bull." Even so, the writer couldn't resist the danger and advised her female readership to immediately get Vespas of their own.

Some scooter clubs became exclusively female, or at least dominated by the sex once perceived as weaker. One of these dangerous dames of the Secret Servix Scootin' Chicks echoed the feminist cry to get off the pillion: "My favorite part of being a scooter girl is convincing those girls on the back of bikes to get their own." In 1997, *Scoot* magazine writer Christian Larsen profiled these new sororities: "Beware, fellow male Vespa and Lambretta riders, some of these girls will out-ride you, out-race you, out-fix you, and out-drink you."

At the same time, the Vespa once again became a fashion and political statement to express female liberation. This followed a long tradition, since Sonia Delaunay painted her Citroën B12 to match her Parisian outfits in 1925 and Milanese stylist Emilio Pucci used a scooter on the fashion runways in 1949. Later Anna Sui "rediscovered" the Vespa on a 1995 catwalk as the ultimate accessory. DIY punk scooterists followed haute couture as *Vogue* ran a huge spread on this "new" Vespa style. The article highlighted women-only scooter clubs with names like the Scheming Bitches Scooter Club, who declared, "We . . . had a rule that our boyfriends couldn't drive our bikes with us on the back."

"BADLY TROUSERED WOMEN"
FASHION FAUX PAS

Scooter riders have always known to never listen to the critics. *Life* magazine pooh-poohed the scooter revolution of the 1950s, referring to the mini cycles as "only a tame plaything in the US." This followed a long tradition going back to a 1938 *Chicago Daily Times* article about Moto-Scoot calling them "puddle-jumpers," "vest-pocket motorcycles," and "powered roller skates." Journalists consistently referred to scooters as "putt-putts," and *Time* magazine gave critics new insults to hurl at scooterists in 1967: "because of their blue crash helmets, scooter men endure such other names as 'blisterheads' and 'bubbleheads.'"

> ## "THIS IS MORE THAN A FAD, IT'S A REVOLUTION."
> ## —THE *NEW YORKER* WARNING OF THE VESPA INVASION, 1957

The difference is that Vespas, unlike motorcycles, aren't threatening. A Piaggio ad from 1964 echoed this sentiment: "If you buy a Vespa, your neighbors don't move out of the neighborhood. The Vespa is a motorscooter, not a motorcycle. There is no social stigma attached to driving one." Vespas are friendly and fun versus dirty, dangerous motorcycles.

Until the Vespa was introduced after World War II, though, scooters often were bizarre-looking contraptions with spot welds and borrowed lawnmower engines. The only product testing was on the unsuspecting general public. "One manufacturer bolts the driver's seat directly to the cylinder head by means of extension rods to save space and to reduce weight," wrote *Popular Mechanics* in 1947 as a strange endorsement for an uncomfortable (and ugly) scooter.

With the Vespa, though, fashion mattered. In 1958, the *New York Times Magazine* understood and declared that the Vespa "is a daring and noisy announcement that its passengers are individualists with a continental flair but without the purchase price of a Continental Mark III."

Fashion designers embraced the Vespa and sewed their clothes to fit this new lifestyle. The new fads inevitably changed to be better for riding. In 1950, *Picture Post* featured the new Vespa rider's look: "The narrowing of the new-look skirt was dictated in order to prevent it getting tangled up with the wheels. The slipper shoe was created for footplate comfort. The turtleneck sweater and neckerchief were designed against draughts on the neck." Sunglasses became a staple of scooter chic as well as keeping bugs out of the rider's eyes.

Trousers were soon the rage, since skirts would inevitably blow back, and a headkerchief kept new hairdos in place. While Piaggio embraced this new wave of style for Vespa riders across the world, its rival in Milan, Innocenti, couldn't stand these fashion faux pas, and its prudish newsletter *Lambretta Notiziario* complained that "one is all too-frequently tormented by the sight of badly trousered women on motor scooters." Vespa saw the future, embraced the new look, and left Lambretta in its dust.

CHAPTER FOUR

IT'S A MOD, MOD WORLD

MOD, MODERN, MODEST
THE BIRTH OF A REBELLION

England in the early 1960s was finally on the upswing after a grueling war, but mum and pop still kept their stiff upper lips and avoided excess. Finally, though, they could perhaps afford a Mini Cooper with the rising standard of living. Their kids hadn't lived through the Battle of Britain and couldn't understand their parents' seriousness and rigid rules for survival. Instead, the younger set wanted to zip over the glistening cobblestone streets at full tilt on a souped-up Vespa or Lambretta. The scooter became a piece of jewelry for mods, with all the flashy mirrors, which complemented the slick Italian clothes, Beatles boots, and mop-top dos. Whereas their parents united together to save Britain and the world, the mods united together to dance and be seen on their high-speed steeds.

Some speculate that the early mods earned their name from modern jazz and grew out of the Beat Generation. Meanwhile the rockers were preceded by the dapper Teddy Boys, or "Teds," which is short for Edwardian, since they borrowed some styling cues from early English Edwardian times.

> "THE MOD WAY OF LIFE CONSISTED OF TOTAL DEVOTION TO LOOKING AND BEING 'COOL,' SPENDING PRACTICALLY ALL YOUR MONEY ON CLOTHES AND ALL YOUR AFTER HOURS IN CLUBS AND DANCE HALLS."
>
> —RICHARD BARNES FROM *MODS*

The Teds outdid each other in their slicked-back hair and patent-leather shoes as they bopped to the music of American rock 'n' roll. Whether these origin stories are true or not, the mods and the rockers represented something shockingly new, a "moral panic" for the rest of the UK, which couldn't understand

why teenagers had to thumb their collective noses at society and rumble on the beaches.

Some mods were pill poppers who downed their "blues" and "purple hearts" to prove that sleep was irrelevant. They "were a little too smart, somewhat too alert, thanks to amphetamines," according to social historian Dick Hebdige. Meanwhile, the rockers numbed their senses in ale before hopping on their café racers to zoom between the Ace Cafe in London and the Busy Bee Cafe in Watford.

The Brit tabloid the *Sunday Mirror* reveled in hyping this wild nightlife with a front-page feature "Exposing the Drug Menace," with a large purple-hearts bottle of Drinamyl. Assuming that all mods were doped up, parents pulled their teenagers from clubs and tried to protect them from this decadence. "Thus pills medically prescribed for the treatment of neuroses were used as ends-in-themselves," wrote Dick Hebdige in *Subculture*. Mods survived the hype and kept their Vespas zooming at full speed to escape the madness.

Most mods came from London's lower-class East End and scrimped and saved for some extra shillings from low-skilled jobs to hit the classy shops on Carnaby Street for the latest Italian styles. Hebdige wrote that mods revered the slick styles from Italy: "He is English by birth, Italian by choice." The Vespa was the ultimate Italian fashion accessory. Imagine the consternation of their elders, who had just successfully defeated the Italian fascists, only to have their offspring imitate these "swarthy" southern Europeans.

The blatant materialism also appalled the older generation, as each purchase turned into a fashion statement and symbol of rebellion. The goal was always to look one's best, one-up one's mates, and ridicule uptight upper-class twits with money to burn by dressing even better than they did. To have cool stuff was to flaunt it. Hebdige wrote that the mods were a "grotesque parody of the aspirations of [their] parents . . . who used goods as 'weapons of exclusion.'" This conspicuous consumption by the mods, whether consciously or not, parodied the older generation's get-rich dreams by making a mockery of the capitalist ethos of commodifying anything. Unfortunately, the mod movement was itself commodified when television shows such as *The Mod Squad* and others adopted the look with little of the message

THE LIFE

(and too few Vespas). While materialism may have been the mod cry for a while, many mods eventually moved on to psychedelics and even hippy principles, which fiercely rejected consumerism.

Some of the earliest mods bowed out when the media "discovered" the movement, and the latest magazines splashed features of the latest stars. Television shows such as *Ready Steady Go!* featured the "with-it" bands of the week, from the Small Faces to the Hollies and an opening shot of a scooter revving its engine when the light turned green. The Who debuted many of their iconic songs on this show, which was broadcast on black-and-white tellies across the land.

Ready Steady Go! marked the official countdown to the weekend. When the whistle blew and the young mods left their dead-end jobs, they kick-started their Vespas and danced all night to northern soul, the Skatalites, or whoever the band of the month happened to be at the Scene Club in London. Now what would the parents say about that?

THE BATTLE OF BRIGHTON
THE ORIGINAL GENERATION X

London tabloid writers were glee-fully outraged. "Mutated locusts wreaking untold havoc on the land!" fumed one columnist, referring of course to "those vermin," the mods. These Vespa-riding teenagers hit the beaches of Brighton for a bank holiday in mid-May 1964 to battle the rockers. "We will fight them on the beach," became the Churchill-mocking rallying cry.

Nineteen sixty-four was a banner year for delinquency, or at least the pleasantly scandalized journalists would have us believe this. That year, California's attorney general fanned the flames with the mostly fabricated and exaggerated report on "Hoodlum Activities." Inside, he explained what to look for in a rebel: "an embroidered patch of a winged skull wearing a motorcycle helmet. . . . Many affect beards and their hair is usually long and unkempt. Some wear a single ear-ring in a pierced ear lobe. . . . Some clubs provide that initiates shall be tattooed. . . . Another patch worn by some members bears the number thirteen." He described the ste-reotype of the motorcycle-riding rocker and natural enemy of the usually younger mods.

Meanwhile, British journalist Jane Deverson interviewed young mods in London to chronicle their rebellious views and horror of stodgy English society. "Religion is for old peo-ple who have given up living," one mod professed. This youth culture mostly rejected its followers' elders by confessing, "Marriage is the only thing that really scares me." The interviews with these mods proved too dodgy for Deverson's maga-zine, *Woman's Own*, especially with quotes like "You want to hit back at all the old geezers who tell us what to do." Instead, she published her portrait of mods in the 1964 semi-nal book *Generation X*, with the "X" referring to the unknown descrip-tor of what this new, lost generation really represented. The title was later coopted by Douglas Coupland for his debut novel and became the name for a new generation.

Deverson and her cowriter, Charles Hamblett, struck a nerve with their book on the mods, espe-cially after the 1964 "Battle of Brighton." Vespa gangs had already taken tours of the beach towns of Clacton and Hastings, but now more than a thousand mods and rockers descended on the seaside

resort of Brighton, blasting exhaust from the Vespas and Lambrettas or their BSAs, Triumphs, and Royal Enfields. Police arrested seventy-six for disturbing the peace and rioting. Margate, another coastal town, saw four hundred youth blast into town, and the bobbies rounded up sixty-four of them to spend time behind bars.

The redtop tabloids elatedly ran banner headlines: "Youngsters Beat Up Town—97 Leather Jacket Arrests," according to the *Daily Express*. The *Daily Mirror* tabloid splashed the headline "Wild Ones Invade Seaside," with a reference to Marlon Brando's fictional, tough rocker in *The Wild One*, even if the British Board of Film Censors had banned that film for being too provocative. The *Daily Telegraph* told of a "Day of Terror by Scooter Groups," and the *Sunday Mirror* ran an exposé about this mod subculture, describing how it "began by experimenting with purple hearts and other pep-pills, then progress via 'reefers' (marijuana) to heroin and cocaine—the two drugs that almost always lead to death before the age of thirty-five." In other words, all the mods would be dead soon, so let them dig their own graves.

> "YOU'D REALLY HATE AN ADULT TO UNDERSTAND YOU. THAT'S THE ONLY THING YOU'VE GOT OVER THEM—THE FACT THAT YOU CAN MYSTIFY AND WORRY THEM."
>
> —SUSAN, A MOD LONDONER QUOTED IN *GENERATION X*, 1964

Piaggio was aghast that its benign scooters had been transformed into a rebel's steed. No longer would Piaggio sponsor any scooter rallies in Britain, since "'social scootering' had formerly summoned up the image of orderly mass rallies," according to Dick Hebdige. "Now it was suddenly linked to a more sinister collective: an army of youth, ostensibly conformist—barely distinguishable as individuals from each other or the

crowd—and yet capable of concerted acts of vandalism."

The seaside tiff between the mods and the rockers only heightened their status. *Generation X* quotes one of the mods at the Margate kerfuffle, John Braden, who looked back fondly at the melee: "It was great—the beach was like a battlefield. It was like we were taking over the country." Even if he was just fighting the rockers, he felt as if he were battling British society and the stodgy geezers. "We just want to show them we're not going to take it."

Youth culture adopted the Vespa as its symbol of freedom and rupture from the classist culture of it's adherents' parents. Just like the Who stuttering, "Hope I die before I get old" in "My Generation," nineteen-year-old David from London told the authors of *Generation X*, "I think old people are ridiculous. So phoney, everything they do is false. I'm rude to my mum and ignore my dad, and that's how it should be."

The Vespa had lost its *Roman Holiday* innocence. Hebdige wrote that after the mod riots "the motor scooter, originally an ultra-respectable means of transport, was turned into a menacing symbol of group solidarity." Ironically, the beachside battles and the tabloid banner headlines only made the Vespa more popular.

ROCKERS!
"LIKE ELVIS, ONLY WORSE"

"You've got to be either a mod or a rocker to mean anything," proclaimed a young mod woman in one of the British tabloids in 1964. The lines were drawn, so while the mods twisted all night and popped pills before hopping on their Vespas, rockers at the Ace Cafe put some pence in the jukebox, hopped on their Nortons, and zoomed a course to race back to the bar before the song stopped.

Rockers mocked the mods as too studied and perfectly groomed, but these British greasers carefully copied American motorcyclists while making the style swankier with a leather jacket, a white T-shirt, and slicked-back hair. "Then comes the scarf. . . . It was stolen from American Cowboy movies," according to Johnny Stuart in his book *Rockers*. "The Rocker begins to take on something of the Cowboy's identity as a wanderer, tramp, hobo; a bit of a villain too."

"Rockers look like Elvis Presley, only worse," complained seventeen-year-old mod Terry Gordon to the *Daily Mirror* in 1964. Indeed, Elvis the Pelvis, with his suggestive shimmies, poofy pompadour,

and too-cool grin, proved an irresistible hero to imitate for the rockers. They had difficulty finding a Harley-Davidson like Elvis's shiny 1956 red-and-white KH model in England, so rockers resorted to souping up BSA Goldstars, Triumphs, or Royal Enfields into jet-propelled café racers.

The mods scorned the rockers right back, and the print media regularly disparaged them as well. "Motorcycle people aren't used to dealing with the general public," *Mechanix Illustrated* wrote in 1956. "Some of them may give you a hard time if you don't look like one of the Wild Ones."

Young Terry Gordon expressed her horror over the trampy rocker floozies in their sleazy fishnet stockings compared to her tasteful friends, who wore prim mod skirts with bobbed haircuts: "Mod girls don't wear any makeup—only foundation. Rocker girls use a lot of bright pink lipstick and piles of makeup."

Motorcyclists couldn't understand why anyone would want to drive a scooter when a much more powerful motorcycle was within reach. In Richard Hough's snobby

introduction to *A History of the World's Motor Cycles,* published in 1966, he takes a moment to denigrate the much more popular Vespa: "The scooter is a device that we refuse to grace with a description of a motor cycle and which, therefore, has no place in this work."

The mods mocked those rockers who obviously had to make up for some deficiency in their manliness by buying more horsepower. Cultural critic Paul Willis followed a similar argument when he wrote about British rockers in Birmingham: "The lack of the helmet allowed long hair to blow freely back into the wind, and this, with the studded and ornamented jackets, and the aggressive style of riding, gave the motorbike boys a fearsome look which amplified the wildness, noise, surprise and intimidation of the motorbike. . . . The high cattlehorn handlebars, the chromium-plated mudguards gave the bikes an exaggerated look of fierce power."

The rockers assumed everyone admired their look. Doesn't everyone want to be covered head to toe in leather, a bandana around the neck or head, and clunky boots? The mods jeered at the unwieldy motorcycles dripping oil with exposed, hot pipes, which could possibly burn the rider.

British motorcycle enthusiasts had been humiliated some years before in 1955 when at the Earl's Court Motor Cycle Show only a few motorcycles were displayed against fifty new scooters and moped models. Befuddled rockers continued to scratch their collective heads at these "Italian hairdryers on wheels." In 1979, author Jack Woods wondered. "Is the Scooter Making a Comeback?" in his article for *Motorcycle Sport* and went on to criticize all scooters as motorcycle wannabes. The only scooter he deemed worthy was the largest one, the gigantic 250cc Maico Mobile, which was more like a covered motorcycle. "It could romp along at a confident 70mph holding the road like a motorcycle," he applauded, while the mods dubbed this bizarre covered motorcycle as a German dustbin.

Woods ended the article extolling the virtues of motorcycles and jabbing Vespas by bragging, "Motorcycling is a much more complex sport than scootering. . . . Motorcycling is fun of a multidimensional variety. Scootering is pleasure of the more superficial sort." And these rockers wondered why the mods loathed them.

VESPA-LAMBRETTA WARS
THE LINES ARE DRAWN

While the mods were hashing it out with the rockers, Piaggio's Vespa battled with Innocenti's Lambretta. Piaggio hailed from Pontedera (near Pisa in Tuscany) and Innocenti from the Lambrate area of Milan, the capital of Lombardy. The Vespa was named for a buzzing wasp, while the Lambretta was a diminutive nickname for the Lambro River, which bubbled by the factory.

Piaggio marketed the Vespa below its rival's price, but the Lambretta faithful, *lambrettisti*, argued that the Milanese scooter was a better machine. The longer wheelbase made for a smoother ride, and its engine seemed faster and more reliable. Lambrettisti criticized the Vespa's slight lean because of the side-mounted engine and the wasp's near-vertical front fork leading to a sinking feeling at a quick stop.

Vespisti just ignored the critics, since they boasted a crucial styling cue: a covered scooter. The earliest Lambrettas looked more like a scooter-moped hybrid, with small floorboards and exposed everything. Piaggio sheathed the motor with side panels, the wheels with fenders, and a generous floorboard that seemed to meld into the headstock. Piaggio's designer, Corradino D'Ascanio, reasoned correctly that

scooter buyers didn't want to see the ugly engine and the metal frame but wanted a beautiful bee to give them wings. No wonder Vespas were far more numerous than Lambrettas. Innocenti finally succumbed to the market and offered its LD as both a covered and uncovered model. While loyal lambrettisti cried foul, the sleek lines of the sheathed Lambretta made it a favorite with fashion-conscious scooterists.

Piaggio spearheaded the Italian scooter invasion into Britain. The Douglas firm began importing Vespas across the English Channel and added a stylized chrome "Douglas" above the Vespa logo on the leg shield. Piaggio soon licensed Douglas to make British-built Vespas, which hit the streets by March 1951. Innocenti preferred to keep the fashionable "Made in Italy" sticker when the Agg family set up a huge distribution network with a massive marketing campaign and many more dealers and repair shops than Douglas Vespa. The stage was set for the Lambretta–Vespa wars.

The mod obsession with the most fashionable model took both of these manufacturers by surprise. To have the latest, fastest, coolest scooter proved irresistible. Vespa showrooms stocked only a few of the imported, speedy GS scooters, which were more expensive to ship, rather than selling a home-bred Douglas Vespa. The Lambretta TV 175 Series 2 earned a reputation as the faster of the two scooters, since window displays would feature only the quickest, most recent models. Innocenti promoted "The Blue Boys," who vowed loyalty to its brand and wore their blue Lambretta Club colors to show that they absolutely would not ride a Vespa. Even BSA, Triumph, and other British motorcycle manufacturers released scooter models to get a share of the market.

The larger Piaggio company, however, released the pinnacle of its classic scooters in 1962: the gorgeous Vespa GS 160. Innocenti responded the next year by releasing its Lambretta GT 200 for the Isle of Man scooter races, which provoked Piaggio's SS120, then Innocenti's SX200, and so on. The mods could only revel in the rivalry of the sleek scooters marketed especially for them.

MOD VESPAS
MIRROR, MIRROR ON THE SCOOTER

Mod Vespas will forever be remembered for the oodles of mirrors and lights jutting from the leg shield like rays from the sun; however, scooter style changed from year to year. Some mods espoused perfect stock scooters, while others hot-rodded the motor and stripped off the side panels to race even the rockers. In the late 1950s, the early post–Teddy Boy/Beatnik phase caught everyone listening to lounge lizards like Monk and Mingus and driving their stock scooters fresh from the crates. As the music changed to the Beatles, the Who, and Otis Redding, so did the decked-out Vespas with every shiny bell, light, and horn that could be attached. Revivalist vespisti have since airbrushed their favorite bands on the leg shields, attached fur trim with leopard-skin seat covers, and dangled a foxtail from the antenna like a cherry on top.

While Piaggio and Innocenti battled for horsepower with their respective Vespas and Lambrettas, the companies also knew that mods loved these aftermarket accessories. One British ad featured plaid seat covers, a windscreen, tartan saddlebags, lots of chrome doodads, and a Lambretta flag that announced "Go Gay!" Innocenti specialized in the two-tone paint scheme on its Lambrettas, which became emblematic of the whole mod movement and ska music. Eddy Grimstead's scooter shop on Barking Road in London claimed it debuted these two-tone scooters, and Piaggio and Lambretta followed suit with styling packages and paint schemes with names such as "Hurricane," "Imperial," "Mona," and "Z-Type."

Certain accessories were all the rage for the moment, while windscreens and flags were deemed passé. Chrome crashbars, lights, and mirrors, however, kept everyone watching. The mod handbook *Empire Made*, released decades after the original movement, said that "these extras would slow the bike down considerably, although this didn't bother mods as speed wasn't their priority, the slower you go, the more people see you."

Most mods could hardly afford to spring for a new scooter every other year, so a few accessories ensured a brand-new look. Vespa side panels were attached with hinges on the side, whereas Lambretta panels could be removed and replaced

with the new look. "For every genuine [Lambretta] GT200 there were several alleged GT200s of dubious origins," according *Empire Made*. Tricksters could start with a Lambretta TV Series 1, which *were* notoriously unreliable, then purchase new side panels, a bench seat, and some chrome. Only a trained eye could determine a scooter's origin.

It didn't help that scooter keys were almost identical, as shown in *Quadrophenia*, when Jimmy swipes Sting's Vespa. The scooters had generally been so customized that everyone knew whose bikes was whose. These scooters were a symbol of individual taste and no longer conformed to what Piaggio had originally envisioned. The factory-made Vespa had been coopted by the mods and transformed through paint and accessories to be a tool of rebellion.

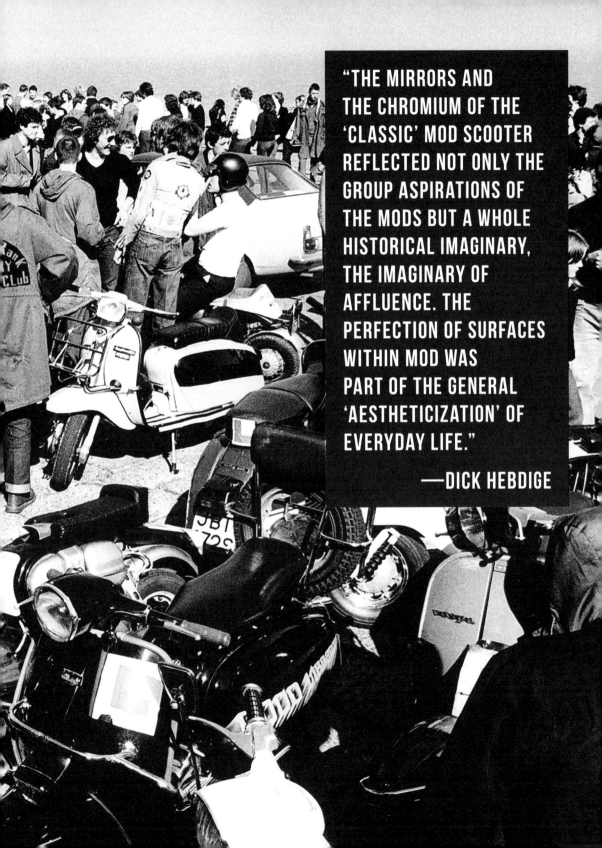

"THE MIRRORS AND THE CHROMIUM OF THE 'CLASSIC' MOD SCOOTER REFLECTED NOT ONLY THE GROUP ASPIRATIONS OF THE MODS BUT A WHOLE HISTORICAL IMAGINARY, THE IMAGINARY OF AFFLUENCE. THE PERFECTION OF SURFACES WITHIN MOD WAS PART OF THE GENERAL 'AESTHETICIZATION' OF EVERYDAY LIFE."

—DICK HEBDIGE

TWO-TONE!

As soon as the press splashed the mods across the front pages and the media cashed in on this new phenomenon, many lamented the death of the mods. "Rock is dead . . . long live rock!" screamed the Who, since reports of its death had been greatly exaggerated.

"Somewhere on the way home from school or work, the mods went 'missing,'" wrote Dick Hebdige. "They were absorbed into a 'noonday underground' of cellar clubs, discotheques, boutiques, and record shops which lay hidden beneath the 'straight world.'" The mod chameleon simply morphed into various other styles since the moderns, by definition, didn't dwell in the past.

Nineteen seventy-nine was the year *Quadrophenia* hit the cinemas and spurred yet another mod revival. The Who sang the soundtrack to the reenactment of the infamous mod–rocker wars, and the struggle rang true for a new generation. "All that greasy hair and dirty clothes," uttered Jimmy in his heavy cockney about a dirty motorcyclist. "It's diabolical. . . . I don't wanna be the same as everybody else. That's why I'm a mod, see?" Although the mods may have looked the same on the

outside, they were something new and dangerous to the status quo.

Quadrophenia struck a nerve and further cemented the image of the pill-popping mod in oversized anoraks to keep off the incessant English rain. This New Wave mostly rejected bands who were once mod, like the Kinks and the Rolling Stones, who had turned into solid rock bands worshipped by slimy rockers. Instead, many of these new mods latched on to a music style imported from Jamaica when young British holiday-goers came back from the Caribbean inspired by the ska and dub reggae of bands like

the Skatalites. Brit bands like the Specials, the English Beat, Selector, and Madness filled dancehalls with the quick treble guitar strummed on the upbeat and Hammond organs plunking out the melody.

These new-wave mods numbered even more than the original movement and had a multiracial following, perhaps due to the wide range of music. As a reflection of the fans, "two-tone" became the ultimate mod description since it described the checkered patterns of clothes, two-tone scooters, the legendary ska record label founded by the Specials keyboardist, and the idea of black and white, Jamaican and British, uniting to dance to the best music seen in decades. Some of these new mods got a bit too philosophical like the 1980s zine *Absolute Beginners*, which professed, "Mod, Modern. It means now, here, us. . . . The black-and-white clothes, the black-and-white kids. . . . Mod means living today, sensing tomorrow, remembering yesterday and all its pain and love. Mod means us. . . . It's not a wonderful life. It's just a life, the only one we have, and we're not going to live a rerun." Really? Most fans of this new wave just wanted to shake their booties to ska and zoom around on a Vespa just like the first wave before them.

Yet another mod wave broke in 1995 with ska bands such as the Mighty, Mighty Bosstones and Let's Go Bowling. Supermodel Linda Evangelista appeared on a classic Lambretta for the fashion line of Anna Sui, who declared, "I looked at early-eighties' mod like the Jam and current bands like Elastica, then mixed all three decades up to make it more today." The earliest mods were left entirely out of the equation. That same year, the *Independent* declared, "This is the third British mod wave." One wave leads to another.

CHAPTER FIVE

VESPA ODDITIES

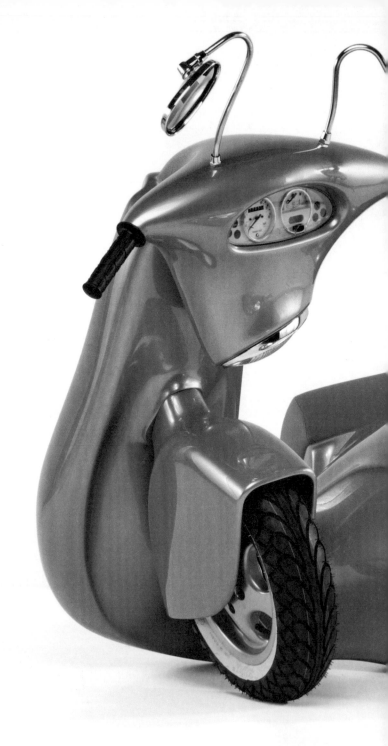

HOLY VESPA!
DIVINE BLESSINGS FROM THE POPE

Celebrations erupted across Italy in April 1956 as the millionth Vespa rolled off the assembly line. Combining the production of all factories in France, England, Germany, and elsewhere that were building Vespas under license, a milestone was reached that even the Holy See couldn't ignore. "Vespa Day" was declared throughout Italy, with festivities held in fifteen Italian cities, the most important one being at the Piaggio headquarters in Pontedera. A convoy of two thousand Vespas traveling en masse through Rome halted all traffic.

Pope Pius XII officially blessed the millionth Vespa on an altar and pushed for more automation for "greater and greater speed to the glory of God." The Vatican viewed the scooter as a means for the masses to get to Mass on time. *Time* magazine wrote about this momentous occasion in 1956 and the papal blessing of this modern chariot: "More people were baptized in 1955; more went to Communion this Easter than ever in history. One reason: motor scooters."

The Church actively advocated for its brethren to use the Vespa to do more good deeds. "Priests in Italy, according to a Vatican report, currently own 30,850 motorscooters, and in terms of sacraments and good works, the average priest's efficiency has climbed to about 3,000 percent over that of his road-trudging 19th century predecessor," according to the *Time* article. "Another straw in this high wind is the decline of the more introverted Benedictines and foot-slogging Franciscans in favor of the fast-moving Jesuits, whose high-octane practicality thrives on the motor-scooter age." Viva la Vespa!

> "MORE PEOPLE WERE BAPTIZED IN 1955; MORE WENT TO COMMUNION THIS EASTER THAN EVER IN HISTORY. ONE REASON: MOTOR SCOOTERS."
>
> —*TIME* MAGAZINE, 1955

The Franciscans' vow of poverty didn't preclude them from owning a Vespa, as *Time* insinuated, since *Life* magazine ran a photo the following year of a Franciscan "Brother Henry" zooming down Baltic Street in Brooklyn dressed in his brown Capuchin monk robe on his Vespa with sidecar, pulling a roller skater.

Although the current pope took the name of San Francesco of Assisi, Pope Francis has yet to be pictured blessing this Italian icon. Nevertheless, Pope John Paul II twice had an audience with the president of the Fédération Internationale des Vespa Clubs, Christa Solbach, and gave his papal blessing to scooterists the world over. Of the sixteen million manufactured, how many are still on the road or have gone to scooter heaven is anyone's guess.

871 KTN

VESPIZZATEVI!
VERBING "VESPA"

Vespa admen knew that hopping on a Vespa would forever change Italian teenagers, who could be freed from the shackles of mamma and papà and allow them to mingle with their peers in the piazza. By altering Dante's beloved Tuscan dialect, Piaggio told Italians to "*Vespizzatevi!*" ("Get Vespa-ed!") and throw off the shackles of the puritanical past. A Vespa was more than just a way of getting town; it was a two-seated matchmaker that would let these hormone-crazed youngsters taste the sweet fruits of youth. In other words, they could now eat the apple of knowledge—and sin.

"Vespa" became a verb to advertising executives who wrote ad copy boasting, "*Chi 'Vespa' mangia le mele (chi non 'Vespa' no).*" In other words, "Whoever 'Vespas' eats the apples (whoever doesn't 'Vespa' doesn't)." Catholic Italy would never be the same, as teenagers could take a bite from the tree of knowledge. Everything a teenager wanted,

sex and sin, were dangling from the apple tree and who cares if they're banished from the Garden of Eden since they can zoom around on a Vespa.

Piaggio knew it couldn't carry the religious symbolism too far for fear of ruffling the feathers of the Church. Still, ad copy advised Vespa buyers to eat "the daisy apple in the meadows." In the local Tuscan dialect, where the Piaggio factory is located, "mela" (apple) also means one's bum, and the plump, curvaceous apple in the ads looked suspiciously like a bulbous buttocks. Suddenly Vespa posters reeked of double entendre when they advised riders to hop on the "the heart apple with one's partner" to admire "the green apple with your head held high" or pursue "the star apple with your headlights on."

The apple ads were a hit, however, despite any fear of the wrath of God from the ads tempting Eve to eat the fruit and experience the beautiful sin of speed. Go ahead, eat the apple!

NO TERRAIN TOO TOUGH
CLIMB EVERY MOUNTAIN, FLY
TO THE CLOUDS!

While the shape of the classic Vespa is unmistakable, the relative simplicity of the design and motor inspired the mechanically minded to "improve" their beloved rides. Bizarre hybrid vehicles—part scooter, part automobile, part airplane (since many spare parts from bombed-out Italian airplane factories found their way onto these little mobiles)—soon zoomed on and off roads. Snow scooters could also be rigged by welding skis on the front for a Vespa-snowmobile crossbreed.

Piaggio made its famous Ape car, a three- or four-wheeled Vespa pickup, to enter the microcar market that boomed briefly in Europe. To capitalize on the Vespa's success, Piaggio marketed a four-wheeled "Vespa car," now a sought-after collector's item. Vespa owners, however, often rigged up their own sidecars or welded on other questionable outriggers for stability and extra passengers.

These multiwheeled "scooters" bridged the gap between the automobile and the Vespa, and even . . . the boat. Perhaps inspired by the millionth Vespa hitting the road in 1956, the English Amanda Water Scooter with a hefty Vincent motor attempted to reestablish the British armada. In one incident, the fiberglass hull melted, causing a breach in the hull, and the test driver drowned. Another attempt to bring scooters to the sea at the 1965 Brighton motorcycle show used a £25 conversion kit for Lambretta scooters that attached paddle blades to the rear wheels, reminiscent of Mark Twain's riverboat years on the Mississippi.

It was finally a Vespa that conquered the waves, much as Julius Caesar crossed the English Channel

> "I'M NOW WORKING ON A COUPLE OF COLLAPSIBLE PONTOONS AND A PROPELLER DRIVE."
>
> —SCOOTER MECHANIC QUOTED IN *POPULAR SCIENCE*, 1961

Vespa Alpha   1967

to spread the Pax Romana. Georges "Jojo" Monneret hooked up his 125cc Vespa to a pair of pontoons with a glorified bathtub in between, which held his scooter upright. The engine powered a little two-blade propeller that pushed the scooter along. His first trial run to reenact William the Conqueror's attack on Britannia failed when he ran into a rascally tree stump. He tried again with a three-blade prop and successfully crossed "la Manche" in five and a half hours—a record never beaten (or attempted) by other scooterists.

Perhaps we'd all have a bit more peace if these precursors to modern jet skis just kept the scooters to the road rather than risking the waves. Soon, though, ambitious Vespa riders wanted to conquer the clouds. *Popular Science* quoted a do-it-yourselfer scooterist in 1961 who announced, "I'm now working on a couple of collapsible pontoons and a propeller drive. So this summer, when I ride the scooter up to the lakeshore, I'll just keep on going. And maybe— souped up a little and equipped with rotor blades—it'll lift off the ground."

OBSTACLE COURSES AND BULLFIGHTING INTENTIONALLY DANGEROUS, BUT WHAT A SIGHT!

Give a boy a bike and he'll ride no-handed and pop wheelies. Give a girl a Vespa and she'll ride a gymkhana course. "Gymkhana" scooter obstacle courses tested riders' agility around orange cones, over wooden teeter-totters, and off jumps. Esso gas stations sponsored these obstacle courses for "professional" Vespa riders—don't try this at home!

"Historians believe the British started them in India. Mounted horsemen of the Bengal Lancers sharpened battle maneuvers by wheeling and turning through obstacles," according to a 1959 Cushman scooter comic that delved into gymkhana's origin. Imagine fighting off Bengal tigers on a Vespa! Well, some scooterists have indeed dressed in full armor and lanced fellow vespisti as a scooter stunt at a rally.

Vespa clubs promoted wild gimmicks at their rallies, such as fitting as many riders on a Vespa as possible. A popular sport on Vespas was scooter polo, which the earliest reference dates back to 1939 in a *Popular Mechanics* article: "a bit faster than bicycle polo, the motorized sport brings occasional spectacular spills, but it's easy to jump off and the injuries to players are few." Strangely, the same magazine ran another piece on this dangerous motorized sport in 1947, declaring it "new": "Scooters have invaded the sporting world and 'scooter polo' has been played as a stunt to large crowds."

Even bigger crowds came out for Vespa bullfighting, as declared by *American Mercury* in 1957: "In Spain, there has emerged a new style comic art. A garishly costumed toreador 'fights' the bull on a Vespa between acts of an orthodox bullfight." Now that's a sport!

Most clubs, however, just stuck to gymkhana courses to test their riding agility and to laugh at the worst accidents, which were usually nothing more than a few scrapes.

TROOPS ON TWO WHEELS
KEEPING THE PEACE

Putting more cops on the beat proved easy by just giving them a Vespa. Soon British bobbies zipped through London on Douglas Vespas to snatch the hooligans. Mexico City had its *fuerzas armadas policiales* on scooters to catch banditos.

No more could sneaky Italian Mafiosi outrun poor carabinieri on their poky Bianchi bicycles. Instead, the notoriously dimwitted carabinieri fought back in 1949 with the Vespa Forze Armate (Vespa Armed Forces) to round up the petty pickpockets ruining visitors' Roman holidays. The cavalry came in with Piaggio's supply of three-wheeled Ape cars to reinforce the *poliziotti*.

In 1967, *Time* poked fun at New York City's attempt to subdue the evildoers in Gotham with its S C R A M B L E patrols, or Scooters in Communication with Range and Mobility for Better Law Enforcement. The magazine mocked the "beefy cops on dainty putt-putts" and called up the cliché of donut-munching cops who needed a Vespa to fight crime. "The putt-putting noise daunts would-be lawbreakers; the potential speed (60 miles per hour) and mobility enable

wheezy cops to outrun juvenile delinquents." Four years later, though, a 1971 United Press International article profiled how a Vespa possibly saved a cop's life when a "New York City policeman ducks behind a police scooter" as dozens "of city policemen, several armed with shotguns, poured into the building." Two people were killed, but not the cop hiding behind the Vespa's leg shield.

Vespa cops would naturally evolve into Vespa troops. Enrico Piaggio halted any such talk since he was fed up with two years of futile discussions with the Italian carabinieri and NATO about using Vespas. "I am ever more convinced that the 'military' are not worth the time of day," he lamented.

Even so, the Finnish Ski Patrol used Vespas across the frozen northern tundra to protect Finland's border from the Soviet Union. The French Foreign Legion stuck a bazooka through a Vespa's leg shield as a secret weapon in its (failed) attempt to hold on to Algeria. "France mounted 75mm cannons on Vespas for mobile troops," reported *American Mercury* in 1957. The kick from a bazooka blast would surely send the driver safely into the ditch.

MISS VESPA DARLING
SCOOTER BEAUTY PAGEANTS

By the mid-1950s, Piaggio was no longer advertising a product; it was promoting a lifestyle.

Piaggio financed massive advertising campaigns to promote "scooter culture" in general, and the Vespa in particular. Rinaldo Piaggio hailed from Genoa, so Vespa advertised that he followed in the footsteps of Christopher Columbus, who also was born in Genoa, for the second conquest of the New World. Piaggio & Co. sponsored international beauty contests, which weren't just about the female driver looking her best but also about how the scooter was tidy and decked out with accessories. In Britain, glamorous movie stars awarded the Silver Rose Bowl to Miss Vespa Darling, to much fanfare.

Vespa magazines funded by Piaggio appeared in several languages with updates on the latest models and rallies and paparazzi shots of celebrities atop sleek scooters. The magazines generally stayed away from grubby mechanical maintenance, instead promoting Vespa culture and the idea of the sleek, attractive scooter that was fashionable but functional. Sure, the practical scooter could tour the world and squeeze through maddening traffic, but this was a stylish steed that removed the gas tank from between the driver's legs and kept clothes clean by covering the dirty engine.

The magazines promoted a new style to keep the female ridership looking its best. "The pocket handkerchief fashion which swept the women's world in 1949 was devised to keep a pillion girl's hair tidy at speed. . . . Next year, the blown hair problem was solved by the urchin cut," *Picture Post* wrote in 1954 in the article "A New Race of Girls."

The ultimate embellishment to the latest trends was, of course, the Vespa. According to Dick Hebdige, "In the early 1960s . . . scooters were displayed (and sometimes sold) not in car or motor-cycle showrooms but in exclusive 'ladies' fashion shops. They were thought to be a good thing to dress a window with, regarded less as a means of transport than as chic metal accessories, as jewellery on wheels." Piaggio had succeeded in making the Vespa more than a scooter; it was now a statement of style, the ultimate decoration.

VESPA BOUTIQUES?
PERFUME AND BATH OIL

Piaggio's Italian invasion into the US brought the Vespa to Sears department-store showrooms right next to the lawn mowers and clothes dryers. Even the classic Vespa decal on the legshield was pried off for an all-American "Allstate" logo surrounded by the borders of the Lower Forty-Eight. The allure of Italian design was lost, and the poor scooters were reduced to a functional toy as opposed to a lifestyle. This ham-handed marketing was nothing new in the American scooter world, as the diminutive Doodlebug was displayed in Gambles five-and-dime stores next to the pogo sticks, Hula-Hoops, and yo-yos as toys for kids. Vespa was falling victim to the same pitfalls. Imports came to a grinding halt in 1984, when Vespa couldn't meet US emission standards and Piaggio fretted about product-liability laws.

The Vespa made a grand return to the United States in 2001 with an updated design and a new marketing pitch. The sleek new design—and hefty price tag—assured that new versions of the classic wasp wouldn't be relegated to the fleet-supply warehouse. "If you don't care about quality or image,

buy a plastic Yamaha scooter. If you want to buy into the Vespa lifestyle, we're the place," said Jim D'Aquila, the co-owner of the Vespa Boutique in downtown Minneapolis, in 2002.

Boutique? The new Vespa showrooms promoted a pampered standard of living that gave leather-clad motorcyclists new fodder for making fun of these "Italian hairdryers." Piaggio sold not just slick Vespa watches and Vespa silver cufflinks but branched off into personal hygiene with Vespa perfume, Vespa bath foams, Vespa herbal cream, Vespa bath oil, and Vespa bath salts (in strawberry, mint, musk, and rose scents). No wonder Diane Sawyer on *Good Morning America* hopped on a new Vespa, declaring on national television, "We're not Hells Angels. We're hell's dorks!"

Scooter writer Jeremy Wilker kindly referred to the fifty-one Vespa boutiques around the US as "the Gap approach" to selling scooters. The scooter mechanics who had resuscitated many incapacitated machines during the Vespa shortage bristled at this new effeminate image. Scooter mechanic Jeremy Liebig, who fixed up old Vespas at his Scooter Lab garage, refused an offer to work at one of the boutiques and preferred to get a little grease under his fingernails repairing classic Vespas.

Soon Vespa clones undercut Piaggio's hefty price tag with the Bajaj, Stella, and other scooters that borrowed Corradino D'Ascanio's classic design. One of the Vespa Boutique owners, Gary Kiese, couldn't give much detail about the new Vespas, but instead unwittingly made the ultimate insult to the mods: "I can answer any questions you have on Ducatis and other Italian motorcycles." Had the rockers won the battle and cashed in on the mods' love of Vespas?

Most of the upscale Vespa boutiques shut their doors after a few years, but Piaggio's push to promote its wares paid off. The new Vespa appeared in dozens of TV ads and was the ride of choice of Hollywood stars such as Jay Leno, Sandra Bullock, Tobey Maguire, Sylvester Stallone, Jerry Seinfeld, Kirsten Dunst, Sarah Jessica Parker, and Robert De Niro. Vespa's grand return to the American market paid off and sparked a new scooter craze across the world.

LIVE MUSIC

HighTide

THE BEATLES

Vespa

Vespa

Vespa

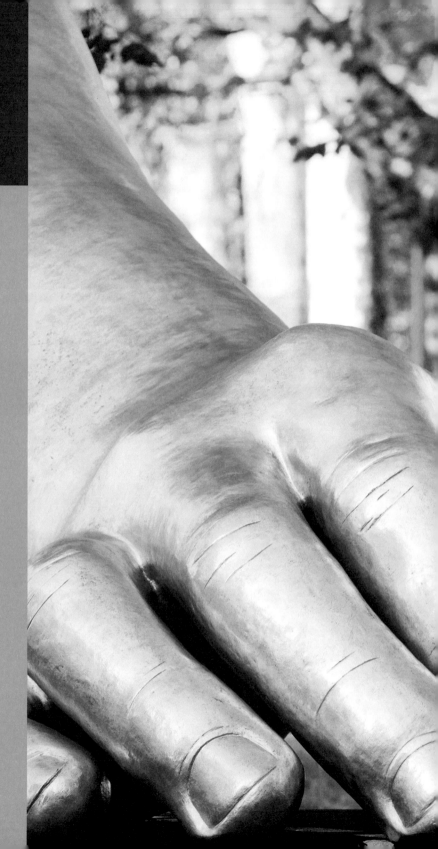

CHAPTER SIX

VESPA IN POP CULTURE

PAPARAZZO!
ROME ON A VESPA

No city has been linked to the magic of the Vespa quite as much as Rome. Who could help falling for Audrey Hepburn on a bulbous Vespa with Gregory Peck behind her on the pillion driving dangerously through traffic around the Eternal City? Director William Wyler scored with his classic *Roman Holiday* in 1953 and started a revolution for Vespas and tourists itching to see the beautiful life in Rome for themselves. To this day, this film still encourages tourists to pay huge fees to rent Vespas to risk life and limb in treacherous Roman traffic. Other films, such as *Three Coins in a Fountain*, tried to catch the magic of Rome but sadly didn't include a Vespa in a starring role.

The next film that caught the essence of Rome, although much darker, was Federico Fellini's *La Dolce Vita*. A phalanx of circling Vespas, and most importantly a scandal photographer named Paparazzo, pursue VIPs on the star-studded Via Veneto. Fellini used the buzzing Vespa to personify the shameless persistence of the media hounds who torment people while pursuing the big scoop. Paparazzo's persistent magnesium flashbulbs blinding his distraught prey have become indelibly engraved on our collective minds, and Fellini gave the world a new word: "paparazzi."

This is a far cry from Gregory Peck's character, who won't reveal that the princess, played by Audrey Hepburn, has gone slumming for the evening. Instead the noble journalist and his photographer sidekick kill the story and give up the photos to the royalty. By contrast, from the naughty newsman played by fantastically cool Marcello Mastroianni, keeps his fair-weather friend Paparazzo around with just enough information to get the exposé. Marcello blasts around Rome in his Triumph Spyder but can never quite escape from the swarm of wasps buzzing around him, encircling his convertible in hopes of getting the scandalous story first. With Paparazzo not far away, Marcello takes part in all-night parties in castles and séances with the fabulously wealthy, and he sleeps with movie stars in prostitutes' beds. Is this really *la dolce vita*, the sweet life? Over seven days in the city of seven hills, Marcello engages in his existential search and ultimate failure to find meaning in all this sweet decadence.

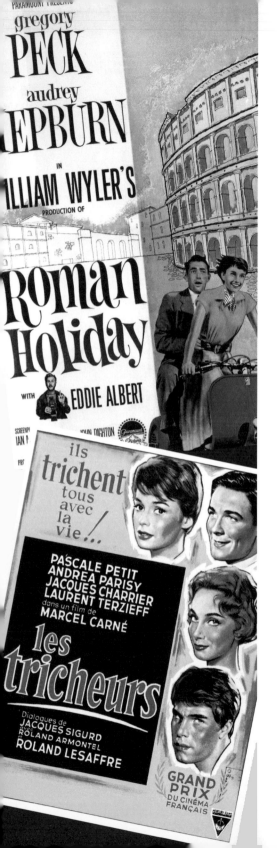

MORE VESPAS ON THE SILVER SCREEN

With the fantastic success of William Wyler's *Roman Holiday* in 1953, Piaggio realized that scooters on the screen provided the marketing coup. Up until this time, the most famous scooter photo of all time was of Amelia Earhart jauntily posing on a Motoped, which suddenly gave the lowly scooter more credibility than any Madison Avenue adman could ever do. Vespas on film—product placement next to glamorous stars—gave them more visibility than any individual photo could possibly achieve.

Piaggio then scored with singer Cliff Richard on a Vespa in the summer-love hit film *Wonderful Life*, but then couldn't stop director Marcel Carné with his 1958 film *Les Tricheurs (The Cheaters)*, in which bandits ride menacing Vespas dangerously down Saint-Germain-des-Prés in Paris with wild bebop screaming in the background. In another film, *Jessica* from 1962, the Vespa helped scandalize Sicily when leggy American midwife Angie Dickinson, on top of her scooter, aroused married men. The jealous Italian women are so disgusted by their drooling Sicilian husbands that they vow to abstain from sex to keep this hussy (and her Vespa) out of their town.

This dangerous, suggestive view of the Vespa could only improve its image, especially when compared with goofy films like *Dick Smart 2007*, which used a Vespa armed with helicopter sails and fins to fly and dive underwater. This gadget-crazy James Bond spoof from 1967 featured a Vespa Super Sport rather than an Aston Martin DB5. The Vespa continued this dive in George Lucas's 1973 *American Graffiti* with the good-natured clown, Terry "Toad" Fields, driving a Vespa GS 160 amid the classic American cars to Mel's Drive-In.

The golden age of American automobiles melded with the golden age of cinema. Even so, many Hollywood celebrities hopped on a Vespa to bask in California sunshine and risk being mobbed by their fans. Paul Newman famously traveled around Israel on a Vespa when he shot *Exodus* in 1960, but this future race-car driver deemed scooters far too risky for his wife, Joanne Woodward. Paparazzi shot photos of dozens of celebrities, from Sandra Dee to Charlie Chaplin, atop Vespas. The trick worked, and even today many movie stars view the Vespa as the ultimate celebrity vehicle to be seen on while zipping down Sunset Boulevard.

DIRTY, FILTHY ROCKERS
HOLLYWOOD EMBRACES THE BULLIES

"American motorcycling's Day of Infamy" took place in the lonely town of Hollister, California, in 1947 when a *Time Life* photographer staged a photo of a member of the Booze Fighters on a Harley acting drunk with emptied beer bottles strewn on the floor. It was a slow news day, but the photo touched a nerve, and panic ensued about these rebels taking over sleepy, small towns. The public outcry demanded a crackdown, and Harley-Davidson was embarrassed. Its motorcycles had just provided exemplary patriotic service to rid the world of fascists and now had become the tool of doped-up rebels?

Hollywood didn't care whether art was imitating life or vice versa, and studios cashed in on the evil, enticing menace. In 1953, the world was shocked—shocked!—when Marlon Brando's gang stormed into a peaceful town, much like Hollister, in *The Wild One* and he met cute Cathy "the square." She's clearly enamored but confused and used to the clean-cut world of Cushman and Salsbury scooters, which promoted a wholesome, productive lifestyle. In trying to understand the boyish but beautiful rebel, Cathy prods Johnny, Marlon Brando's character: "What do you do? I mean, do you just ride around or do you go on some sort of picnic or something?"

Johnny is appalled. "A picnic? Man, you are too square. I have to straighten you out. Now listen, you don't go any one special place, that's cornball style. You just go!" He snaps his fingers as if to wake her up from her suburban slumber. "A bunch gets together after all week. It builds up. The idea is to have a ball. Now, if you gonna stay cool, you gotta wail. You gotta put something down. You gotta make some jive. Don't you know what I'm talking about?"

Clearly she has no idea exactly what this gibberish means, nor did audiences, but it certainly sounds exciting. Cathy is then transformed with just one spin on the back of Brando's bike: "I've never ridden on a motorcycle before. It's fast. It scared me, but I forgot everything. It felt good."

The rockers were born, even if their reason for being was unclear. When Brando's character is asked, "Hey, Johnny, what are you rebelling against?"

"Whatta ya got?" the Wild One responds, as if he's open to anything.

This aimless agitation sets the stage for 1955's *Rebel without a Cause*. Even if this is not a rocker film, since James Dean drives a 1949 Mercury rather than his usual CZ or Royal Enfield motorcycles, this is the first film of hoodlums targeting a scooterist. A gang of bullies, including a teenaged Dennis Hopper, harasses poor Plato on his classic Salsbury 72 scooter as he struggles to escape. Even though Plato is no saint—he shot a litter of puppies—we still relate to his struggle against these dirty rockers.

Off screen, James Dean became a symbol of cool for rockers as he donned his leather jacket, slicked back his hair, and made space on his Triumph motorcycle for blonde bombshell Ursula Andress. Dean wanted speed at all costs and graduated to racing Porsches, which led to his grim demise. At the time Dean died, smashing his Porsche into a lowly Ford, Ursula Andress had already moved on to date the original Hollywood rocker, Marlon Brando. To add insult to injury, she appeared in a cheesecake calendar spread wearing only a leopard-skin coat and sitting atop a baby-blue Vespa.

THE WHO FILMS PRESENT

QUADROPHENIA

A FILM BY FRANC RODDAM

QUADROPHENIA
ROCK 'N' ROLL AND MOD LIT

Music, film, and books all tried to capture the essence of this Vespa revolution. Before the mods were splashed across the front pages of tabloids or lionized on the silver screen, Colin MacInnes wrote *Absolute Beginners* in 1959, which, more than any other book, captured the spirit of Soho and Carnaby Street in London at the birth of the mod revolution. "You could see everywhere the signs of the un-silent teenage revolution," MacInnes wrote of teenaged life. "The disc shops with those lovely sleeves set in their windows and the kids inside them purchasing guitars or spending fortunes on the songs of the Top Twenty. The shirt-stores and bra-stores with cine-star photos in their windows, selling exclusive teenage drag. . . . Scooters and bubble-cars driven madly down the roads by kids, who, a few years ago, were pushing toy ones on the pavement."

These new "modernists" or "mods" listened to modern jazz and bebop rather than the old-fashioned jazz or the cheesy lounge music of Frank Sinatra and his ilk. MacInnes described the scene: "These were beatniks with style who filled the coffee shops through the night after the pubs closed at 11 p.m." In honor of this seminal book, David Bowie signed on to a film adaptation. Bowie earned his chops as a mod in the band Davie Jones with the King-Bees, so he had the credentials to pull off the movie. The 1986 film version of *Absolute Beginners* wisely featured a pristine Vespa as the star of the show, but even Bowie's title-track song and screen presence couldn't save the thin plot.

Even if the film didn't do the book justice, society was suffering from a 1970s culture of platform boots, afros, the Hustle, and the glam-metal band Montrose, with its hard-rocking hit "Bad Motor Scooter." The roaring Vespa engine in the song's lead-in came from an open guitar tuning and a distortion fuzz box: "Get on your bad motor scooter and ride / When the sun comes up, everything gonna be all right."

How did the Vespa get appropriated by Sammy Hagar? Thankfully Pete Townshend and the Who saved the scooter with the best Vespa film ever: *Quadrophenia*. A Vespa graced the album cover as well as the movie poster for this rock opera about the mod–rocker clashes in 1960s

England. Thankfully, the band stays out of the film—perhaps they learned the hard way after the cringe-worthy *Tommy*. Instead, primped mods on Vespas and Lambrettas battle the naughty rockers on BSAs to the blasting sound of Townshend's bowling ball strums on his wailing Rickenbacker amplified by his Hiwatt stacks.

To this perfect soundtrack, the angry, confused mod Jimmy rides his Lambretta laden with a dozen mirrors. Jimmy searches for a better life and someone to admire. He discovers his hero, "Ace Face," played by Sting, is a nothing but poser, a subservient bellboy groveling for tips. The same year *Quadrophenia* hit the theaters, 1979, punk broke on the scene. Suddenly, this mod-revival film made Johnny Rotten and the Sex Pistols look like rebellious dilettantes in search of attention. The film ends with Jimmy stealing Sting's Vespa and driving it off the White Cliffs of Dover, where it sinks into the English Channel.

"I RIDE A GS WITH MY HAIR CUT NEAT / WEAR MY WARTIME COAT IN THE WIND AND SLEET."

—THE WHO, "I'VE HAD ENOUGH," ALSO KNOWN AS "LOVE REIGN O'ER ME"

ARTISTS AND THEIR VESPAS
SCOOTER AS PALETTE

To artists, the Vespa is a canvas. Its wide front leg shield, its bulbous side panels, and its rounded fenders give artists the chance to realize their own ideas on a background that is already a piece of art. Art on art.

Decorating vehicles extends back to the earliest transportation. Archaeologists uncovered King Tut's gold-covered chariot to haul him along the Nile, and the Vikings carved magnificent carriages for their queens. BMW even hired Andy Warhol, Frank Stella, Alexander Calder, and Roy Lichtenstein to paint one-of-a-kind vehicles, which could only end up in a museum. Improving on a Vespa, however, required a certain amount of courage by artists who thought they could enhance the factory finish.

Spaniard Salvador Dalí was recognized as the first to add his signature to a Vespa side panel, as if the act of signing it somehow made the scooter his own creation. Perhaps Dalí wanted to raise the same furor that Marcel Duchamp caused when he made a "readymade" piece of art by simply adding his signature (a

> "HOW BEAUTIFUL IT IS TO GO AROUND / WITH WINGS UNDER YOUR FEET / ON A VESPA SPECIAL / THAT TAKES AWAY YOUR PROBLEMS."
>
> —"[VESPA] 50 SPECIAL" BY LUNAPOP

pseudonym) to a urinal and putting it on display. Even though Corradino D'Ascanio is clearly recognized as the designer of the Vespa, Dalí nonchalantly took credit for the Vespa in a flagrant act of comic plagiarism. Dalí had already signed dozens of unpainted canvasses for amateur painters to create their own "original" Dalí and mock the art world collectors. It's too bad Piaggio never turned it back on the artist by creating a *Persistence of Memory* surrealist scooter of Dalí's clocks.

Dalí may be credited with one of the first art scooters, but now many other artists have followed suit. Several Mondrian Vespas with black outlined squares and primary colors zoom around. Besides just painting a Vespa, some artists employ découpage to glue outside images onto the metal. Crafters even "yarn-bomb" Vespas by covering the metallic scooter with a colorful wool sweater. Leopard-skin Vespas prowl the urban jungles, and some Vespas have grass and flowers growing over them as perfect suburban camouflage that would make Picasso green. Perhaps the most striking of all is a creation by Carlos Alberto, a Portuguese artist who made an entire body of a Vespa out of hardwood. The only catch is the little motor won't make this masterpiece a racer too. Art needn't speed.

CHAPTER SEVEN

VESPA CONQUERS THE WORLD

SOVIET SPIES STEAL SCOOTERS THE RUSSIAN VESPA . . . UMM . . . "VYATKA"

When the Iron Curtain bisected Europe during the Cold War, sneaky Soviets infiltrated the West in search of new ideas for the Motherland. Enrico Piaggio made no secret of his contempt for communism and his belief that owning a Vespa was an act of defiance against the majority communists in Italy and further east. Imagine his surprise when the Russian daily newspaper *Izvestia* and the Czechoslovakian automotive magazine *Svět motorů* both featured a fantastic new product that only the Eastern Bloc could dream up: the Vyatka, a scooter clone of the Vespa. Of course this was hardly the first time that "inventors" copied Western designs and hid their pirated products behind a border.

Soviet agents had kidnapped this Italian-made Vespa and smuggled the poor thing deep into the USSR Imagine the confiscated Vespa disassembled under bright lights to find out what makes this little scooter so ingenious. Each piece was meticulously copied, and sometimes improved, to fill the often vacant stores on the other side of the Berlin Wall. The electrical system was enhanced with a larger headlamp in front, but the Russian designers overbuilt the frame in search of a more solid, albeit clunky, ride to withstand the potholes when cruising through Siberia. These Soviet schematics missed the beauty of the lightweight Vespa that put wings under scooterists' feet.

Fifty thousand of the Vyatka were reportedly produced every year, although statistics by a government-controlled press likely exaggerated production numbers. The Italians couldn't retaliate against the nuclear-armed Russian Duma and fumed that royalties from the Vyatka went to finance the wrong side of the Cold War. Even the French newspapers complained about the Soviet scooter scandal as if the French themselves had been harmed: "The Vyatka is nothing but a cheap copy of the French Vespa [sic]." Now . . . who invented the Vespa?

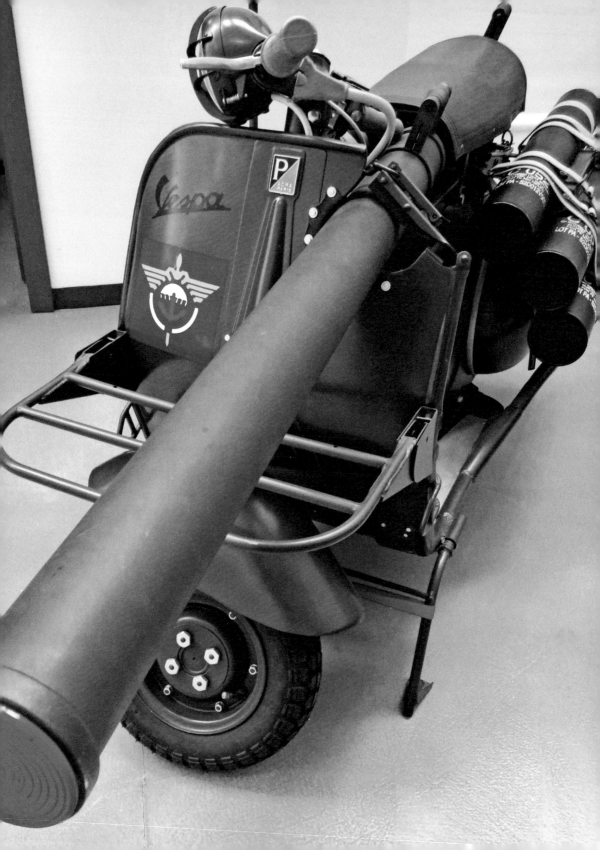

FOREIGN VESPAS
DEUTSCHE, FRANÇAISES, BRITISH, AND BEYOND

Piaggio's factory in Pontedera, Italy, could pump out five hundred scooters a day, but the international market demanded more. Piaggio scanned the possibilities. Germany may be credited with the first motorcycle—Gottlieb Daimler of Kannstatt, Germany, in 1885—but scooter production had to be imported. Just four years after World War II, construction of Vespas reached Deutschland. Production lines near Düsseldorf in Lindorf at the Hoffmann factory made beautiful Die Königin Vespas, but six year later production moved to the former Luftwaffe supplier, Messerschmitt, near Augsburg, Germany. With a downturn of German scooter sales in 1963, Piaggio took production back to Italy and ended the German licensing agreement.

The Italian invasion into Britain happened a bit differently. Englishman Claude McCormack went on a Roman holiday in 1948. While other tourists were cursing those dang scooters ruining their snapshots, McCormack had an epiphany. By the next year, a scooter with

"Douglas" script written above the classic Vespa logo appeared on a pedestal at the Earls Court Motor Show in London. Soon, British holidaygoers no longer needed to venture to the stifling Mediterranean for a spin on a Vespa—or to hear the blasting two-stroke engines keeping them awake. Italian scooters were a smash hit in the UK, so much so that the nobility weighed in with a Royal Warrant in 1967 that heralded, "These are to certify that by direction of His Royal Highness The Prince Philip, Duke of Edinburgh, I have appointed Douglas (Kingswood) Ltd. into the place and quality of Suppliers of Vespa Scooters to His Royal Highness."

Champs-Elysées a decade before. When the Vespas invaded, French pride demanded the Italian scooters be manufactured on native soil under contract by Ateliers de Construction de Motocycles et d'Accessoires (ACMA). The smaller 50cc Vespinas were insultingly classified as mopeds and French law required humiliating bicycle pedals to be added to make it similar to the classic French VéloSoleX. Due to local safety requirements, the headlamp was moved from the front fender to the handlebars—a change that Piaggio soon incorporated into all its Vespas. From 1953 to 1962, ACMA, produced more than one hundred thousand Vespas.

Piaggio's European production marked just the beginning as Vespa construction eventually spread to thirteen countries, including India, Brazil, and Spain. Indeed the little scooter conquered the world.

"Have yo...
say befor...
sentence ...

...dancing will have the new look as ballrooms become
...traps for couples who aren't light on their wheels.

...will become so lazy, they won't even walk from
...oor to the garage for the car; they'll scooter.

...ill be carried everywhere, hanging from
...mily car like a dinghy on a motor yacht.

...w up in this lazy, self-indulgent world,
...o scooter instead of learning to walk.

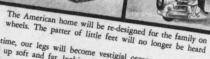

The American home will be re-designed for the family on
wheels. The patter of little feet will no longer be heard

In time, our legs will become vestigial organs, and we'll
end up soft and fat, looking like round-bottom toy dolls.

around the house. Instead, we'll hear the screeching o...
brakes and the clatter of engines as walking disappears...

And round-bottom toy dolls, like the Romans, will be ea...
push-overs for the lean, hungry barbarians from the Ea...

THE GRAND TOUR . . . SPOILED!
VESPA SOUNDING "LIKE RIVETING GUNS"!

Any educated aristocrat in the eighteenth and nineteenth centuries took the Grand Tour of Italy—Venice, Florence, Rome, and Naples—but the Vespa changed everything. Not only did the little wasp allow anyone to travel to these towns, but the buzzing motor made the erudite snobs plug their ears in disgust. *Fortune* magazine complained in August 1956, when six hundred thousand scooters zoomed around Italian roads, that "among Italy's contributions to civilization, the motor scooter cannot be counted as an unmixed blessing. A visitor to Florence, for example, may be lulled to sleep by the strains of La Tosca emanating from the municipal opera house but he is in for a rude awakening when the opera lets out. Indeed, the noise made by a thousand homeward-bound Florentines, most of them riding motor scooters that sound like riveting guns, is enough to drive a tourist back to New York for a little peace and quiet."

These cultural tourists to the *bel paese* (beautiful country) of Italy clearly didn't care about the Vespa's crucial role helping to revitalize a war-torn country. They loathed the idea of these hordes of Vespas, like swarms of wasps, ruining their snapshots in front of the Colosseum and the Trevi Fountain. Rome was ruined! Even quaint hill towns that rarely saw outsiders were no longer so remote and picturesque as buzzing Vespas braved the cobblestones of the town piazza and woke up everyone during naptime. *American Mercury* reported in 1957 that "where ever donkeys go, the Vespa goes too." The Vespa was the perfect vehicle to squeeze into narrow alleys, at least until families could afford a full-fledged FIAT 500.

The snooty tourist tradition continued as Catherine Sabino complained bitterly in her 1988 book, *Italian Country*, that these scooters have destroyed her precious Umbria: "Passageways an arm's length in width will never hear the rumble of an automobile, or with any luck, the irritating buzz of the Vespa." No wonder teenagers saw off the end of the muffler to wake up the tourists!

Fortune in 1956 warned that this Italian invention that had destroyed Old World Italy now threatened the New World with exports of its Vespa: "Now it appears that Americans won't be able to escape motor scooters even by staying home . . . The prospect is in a literal sense disquieting."

THE MECHANICAL BEAUTY OF MOTORS
MOVEMENT EQUALS HAPPINESS

Piaggio soon realized that its Vespa had become a symbol of freedom—a freedom of movement and of no longer being restricted to just walking or relying on public transportation. Suddenly scooterists could venture anywhere in the world, and the Vespa would break their shackles. French philosopher Jean Baudrillard might as well have been discussing the joy of self-determination on a Vespa when he wrote, "Movement alone is the basis of some sort of happiness, but the mechanical euphoria associated with speed is something else altogether, grounded for the imagination in the miracle of motion. Effortless mobility entails a kind of pleasure that is unrealistic, a kind of suspension of existence, a kind of absence of responsibility."

Up until this time, the scooter had been advertised as a "cheaper than shoe leather" transport for salesmen and families. Piaggio advertised its scooter as simply practical in 1964: "The Vespa is a reliable piece of machinery. Its engine has only three moving parts. There's not much that can break. (People have driven Vespas over 100,000 miles without major repairs.) And it's so simple to work on, a complete tune-up costs six

dollars." The company didn't seem to realize that its Vespa had started a revolution and was more than a simple utilitarian piece of equipment.

Perhaps Piaggio wanted its customers to absorb the Vespa's simple, mechanical beauty, much as Robert Pirsig did in *Zen and the Art of Motorcycle Maintenance* when he defended the idea of understanding the perfection of a motor to critics who just wanted the damn thing to

"HATRED OF TECHNOLOGY IS SELF-DEFEATING. . . . TO THINK OTHERWISE IS TO DEMEAN THE BUDDHA."

—ROBERT PIRSIG IN *ZEN AND THE ART OF MOTORCYCLE MAINTENANCE*

run: "I disagree with them about cycle maintenance, but not because I am out of sympathy with their feelings about technology. I just think that their flight from and hatred of technology is self-defeating. The Buddha, the Godhead, resides quite as comfortably in the circuits of a digital computer or the gears of a cycle transmission as he does at the top of a mountain or in the petals of a flower. To think otherwise is to demean the Buddha—which is to demean oneself."

Piaggio tried to prove that the Vespa was indeed reliable and not some little toy by begging Lancia to display the scooter alongside its slick Italian automobiles. Piaggio didn't have the wide distribution and showrooms in its early years in the scooter business, so Lancia filled the void. The result on the Italian mindset was to associate this new "wasp" scooter with the reliability, style, and speed of Lancia.

Once the Vespa was a success, Piaggio struck back at the auto industry in 1964, arguing that a scooter makes more sense. "Maybe your second car shouldn't be a car. Don't laugh, it makes a lot more sense to hop on a Vespa than it does to climb in a 4,000-lb. automobile to go half a mile for a 4-oz. pack of cigarettes."

The comparative safety of an automobile versus a scooter was conveniently skirted. I asked a friend in Modena, the land of Lamborghini, Maserati, and Ferrari, about how safe these vehicles are. "Safe? We don't have this word in Italian. We say *sicuro*, but that's 'secure.' Nothing can be 'safe' because everything is dangerous." Clearly, these are not the people you want driving your taxicab or giving advice on scooter safety.

When Piaggio introduced its Vespa into America, Cushman was already king of the market and had an equally thrilling, if risky, scooter to drive. Product-liability laws were science fiction, and it was left to the media to warn consumers of the danger in scootering. Instead, Piaggio pushed the concept of mechanical beauty inherent in a speeding Vespa, even if most riders wanted to throw caution to the wind and indulge in their wanderlust to travel carelessly across the Old and New Worlds.

VESPA RAIDS
CROSS THAT CONTINENT!

Now free to roam on two wheels, Vespa riders amassed for cross-country tours called "raids." Of course the locals—or the police—may not have been thrilled by the arrival of a buzzing gang followed by a befouling cloud of two-stroke exhaust, but who wouldn't admire the spirit of these brave scooterists willing to traverse the world on a little wasp?

The newfound independence bestowed upon Vespa riders urged them off of the gymkhana obstacle courses to climb mountains, traverse continents, and attach pontoons to a scooter to cross the English Channel—and naturally made for splendid publicity for Piaggio when news spread that a Vespa climbed Mount Snowdon in Wales and that brave vespisti traveled from Milan to the Arctic Circle. The scooter shrank distances and brought people together around the world; spectators cheered or gaped when a traveling Vespa survived the journey to remote landscapes.

These dangerous raids led to believe-it-or-not travelogues of survival of the best mechanic. For example, a Daniel Sauvage put 15,500 miles

on his Vespa traveling around the Mediterranean with his wife on the pillion and wrote *Ma Vespa, ma femme et moi* in 1956 (notice that the Vespa came before his wife in the title). The next year a Belgian photographer, Victor Englebert, upped the ante by venturing due south from Brussels to Cape Town, South Africa. Peter Moore chronicled his search for la dolce vita in Italy, with the clever play on E. M. Forster's novel, in *Vroom with a View* in 2011.

Stories started to circulate about ever more daring trips atop a Vespa. One came from a French soldier who was so fed up with France's debacle in Indochina that he went AWOL armed only with his Vespa. He left the hopeless war against the Viet Minh—US troops would replace the fed-up French in this southeast Asian quagmire—and fled across some of the most rugged terrain in the world on his Vespa just to make it home to France.

The award for most remarkable raid, however, goes to Harry Roskolenko, who set out from Paris to New York (via Kolhapur and Kalgoorlie) on the first round-the-world trip on a scooter beginning on January 3,

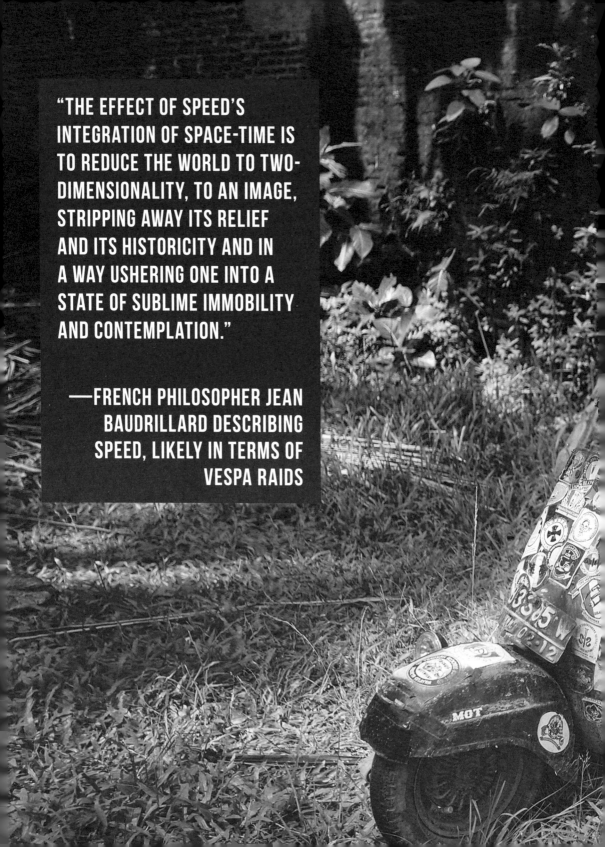

"THE EFFECT OF SPEED'S
INTEGRATION OF SPACE-TIME IS
TO REDUCE THE WORLD TO TWO-
DIMENSIONALITY, TO AN IMAGE,
STRIPPING AWAY ITS RELIEF
AND ITS HISTORICITY AND IN
A WAY USHERING ONE INTO A
STATE OF SUBLIME IMMOBILITY
AND CONTEMPLATION."

—FRENCH PHILOSOPHER JEAN
BAUDRILLARD DESCRIBING
SPEED, LIKELY IN TERMS OF
VESPA RAIDS

1956. "I would be king of the scooter, an emperor of ruts, the prince of the open country and the servant of my own eyes and spirit," Roskolenko wrote in *Poet on a Scooter*. Soon enough, he was in trouble: "One night, in the high mountains of Turkish Kurdistan, I used my Vespa engine to fight off a pack of wolves . . . aiming the scooter's exhaust out toward the pack, again I started the motor, revving it up and exploding it like a machine gun. I had found a weapon, a powerful noisemaker, but a weapon which could kill me too with its fumes. It exploded its furies whenever I revved it up—but what if the spark plug fouled or the fuel ran out? . . . With the scooter's exhaust holding the wolves at bay, I stood there, thinking, praying, freezing yet soaked in sweat, and when the fumes became too strong, I cut the motor down for a few moments, peering at the pack through the darkness to judge their reaction, listening to their howling, then revving, revving, revving, revving, all through the four-letter night."

He survived the wolf pack and a near-marriage experience in Iran to arrive victorious in New York. "I had spent ninety-seven dollars on fuel," he wrote at the end of the trip. "I had traveled 37,000 miles, 21,000 of them by scooter, on the folkways and byways of the world." Piaggio was listening, and soon Vespa raids made headlines across the world and practically become their own genre of nonfiction: the scooter story.

PAGE 6-7

Teens hanging out in Naples, Italy, in 1987 on 50cc Vespas, which speed-crazed fourteen-year-olds could drive according to Italian law since they required no license plate. Mostly, the "Vespina," or little 50cc Vespa, was a means to go to the *piazza* to hang out with friends and the scooter seat conveniently doubled as a bench.

PAGE 8-9

Mod teenagers get ready to ride in Britain. The two Lambretta riders on the right admire the Vespa on the left, so much so that the middle Lambretta even has "GS" stickers on its front legshield, which was only a Vespa model.

PAGE 18-19

Just as policemen used scooters to catch crooks, so did these postmen speed their delivery through snow,

rain, heat, or gloom of night. These classic Autopeds sped along American dirt roads, sidewalks and boardwalks long before Piaggio developed the Vespa with its comfortable seat.

PAGE 22-23

Benito Mussolini (in the hat) stands behind the giant anvil-shaped podium and in front of a giant fasces, the Etruscan/Roman/Fascist symbol of many sticks uniting to be more powerful together with an axe thrown in to quash any resistance. FIAT produced one of the earliest Italian scooters in 1938 and, many years later, the Agnelli family bought Piaggio.

PAGE 58-59

This 1952 photo shows a German beauty sporting an Edelweiss medallion sitting sidesaddle and cross-legged with her hand boldly in her pockets. Never mind that she'll tumble off the back as soon as the driver pops the clutch.

PAGE 70-71

Sardinian singer Marissa Sannia shows off her teen-age style with her white boots, postman's cap, and, most importantly, her 90cc Super Sport, arguably one of the coolest Vespas ever.

PAGE 80-81

The British Mod movement spread overseas and continues to be revived. In this photo, Swedish scooterists clog the streets of Stockholm on St. Erik's Bridge in a Mods vs. Rockers party in 2016—with none of the casualties of the beach battles in Brighton and Margate.

PAGE 84-85

Just as Swedish actress Anita Ekberg would wow Marcello Mastroianni in *La Dolce Vita* from 1960, American actress Mamie Van Doren hops on a Vespa two years earlier in Italy to get the boys' attention with her bleach-blonde hair.

PAGE 86-87

Italian actress Gina Lollobrigida showed the English true Italian style when she visited the Great Film Garden Party here in 1952 in Surrey atop a gleaming open-handlebar Vespa.

PAGE 90-91

To promote safe scootering, the Vespa Club d'Italia organized large rallies and even this women's-only race in 1953 over the washboard stone roads of small town Italy.

PAGE 96-97

Mods goof off outside the Scene Club in London in 1962. Notice the smoking young lad on the pillion seat of the Lambretta while his date does the driving.

PAGE 100-101

The prim mod style, as shown here in a 1966 shot in Wellington in Somerset, stands in stark contrast to the leather and bandana look of the rockers.

PAGE 106-107

The Small Faces show their outrageous style in this 1965 portrait of the original line-up. Kenney Jones (left) would eventually take Keith Moon's place at the drums for The Who, while Rod Stewart and Ronnie Wood would later join the group.

PAGE 116-117

Not all rockers and mods were sworn enemies, as shown in this 1964 photo on English roads. Clearly the café racers of the generally older rockers could easily pass the relatively sluggish scooters, but who looks cooler?

PAGE 128-129

Who's the fairest of them all? One of the most enduring images of the mods are the mirror-laden Vespas, as shown here in 1983 by mod revivalist seventeen-year-old Bryn Owen with his 34 mirrors and 81 lights.

PAGE 138-139

A striking piece from Australian visual artist Patricia Piccini. Nest, 2006 • Fibreglass, auto paint, leather, steel, polycarbonate 90 x 150 x 170cm • Courtesy of the Artist, and Tolarno, Roslyn Oxley9 and Hosfelt Galleries

PAGE 140-141

A Lambretta LD assists the sick as Father Giovanni Antonelli and a fellow priest zoom through the Italian countryside in 1952. The pope officially blessed scooters as a way to spread the Word.

PAGE 150-151

A scooter sightseeing trip on the Thames on a 1965 Lambretta conversion kit with pontoons that made its debut at the 1965 Brighton motorcycle show.

PAGE 162-163

Miss Automobile, Lydiane Huet, waves to the camera from atop a collectible Vespa 400 car with suicide doors at Salon de l'Auto at the Grand Palais in Paris in 1960.

PAGE 164-165

The creator of the Vespa, Corradino D'Ascanio, made his scooter especially with women in mind, as seen in this 1955 line-up. The step-through design, the easy hand shifting, and the maneuverable little wheels spurred the emancipation of women in Italy.

PAGE 194-195

Vespa illustrations by Richard Pettifer, DoubleGood.co.uk

PAGE 204-205

Mad Magazine's Dave Berg thought the scootermania sweeping across the US in the 1950s heralded a new age of laziness. His comic "America is Getting Soft" first appeared in 1958 to show how Americans wouldn't even walk to their cars anymore, but preferred to scoot. He mocked the idea of scooter polo, a sport which he didn't realize had already been played on Salsbury scooters.

PAGE 210-211

Old Vespas never die, but are reincarnated as hotrods as shown in this 2015 shot from Bali in Indonesia.

PHOTO CREDITS

ALAMY STOCK PHOTO

Page 9, Trinity Mirror/Mirrorpix; 12, charles taylor; 14–15, colaimages; 22, Realy Easy Star; 23, Everett Collection, Inc.; 62–63, Rachel Carbonell; 101, David Bagnall; 129, Trinity Mirror/Mirrorpix; 130–131, Andrew Cawley; 137, Nick Moore; 148–149, INTERFOTO; 152–153, image-BROKER; 168–169, Bax Walker; 170–171, Mim Friday; 174 top, Pictorial Press Ltd; 174 bottom, Everett Collection, Inc.; 175 top Everett Collection, Inc; 175 bottom, Photo 12; 176–177, United Archives GmbH; 179, Moviestore collection Ltd.; 180–181, cineclassico; 184, AF archive; 186–187, Findlay; 188–189, AF archive; 190–191, AF Archive; 194, Ryan Barrett; 195, double w; 196–197, raphael salzedo; 207, TiConUno s.r.l.; 208–209, Shahar Shabtai; 212–213, Neil Setchfield; 224–225, paul prescott; 226–227, Trinity Mirror/Mirrorpix; 232–233, Wil Wardle

AUTHOR COLLECTION

Pages 154–154, 193, 201, 202

BRIDGEMAN IMAGES

Pages 16-17, Mods et Teddy Boy; 21, Underwood Archives/UIG; 27, Pierluigi Praturlon/Reporters Associati & Archivi/Mondadori Portfolio; 28–29, SZ Photo/Gert Mähler; 38–39, Pierluigi Praturlon/Reporters Associati & Archivi/Mondadori Portfolio; 40–41, SZ Photo/Gert Mähler; 47, The Advertising Archives; 48–49, Pierluigi Praturlon/Reporters Associati & Archivi/Mondadori Portfolio; 50, The Advertising Archives; 51, PVDE; 52–53, Alinari; 59, SZ Photo/Hannes Betzler; 66–67, SZ Photo/Gert Mähler; 71, Mondadori Portfolio; 82, The Advertising Archives; 84, Pierluigi Praturlon/Reporters Associati & Archivi/Mondadori Portfolio; 89, Manx Press Pictures; 90–91, Mondadori Portfolio; 124–124, DaTo Images; 146, Mondadori Portfolio/Sergio del Grande; 162, AGIP; 182, Pierluigi Praturlon/Reporters Associati & Archivi/Mondadori Portfolio; 183, Pierluigi Praturlon/Reporters Associati & Archivi/Mondadori Portfolio

FOTOLIBRA

Page 153, Derek Metson

GETTY IMAGES

Pages 10–11, Virginia Turbett/Redferns; 24–25, Dmitri Kessel/The LIFE Picture Collection; 30, Keystone Features/Hulton Archive; 32–33, Fototeca Gilardi; 34–35, Keystone-France/Gamma Keystone; 37, Keystone-France/Gamma Keystone; 42–43, David Lees/Corbis Historical; 54, Harry Todd/Fox Photos; 60–61, Keystone-France/Gamma Keystone; 68–69, Popperfoto; 74–75, Dan Kitwood; 79, Paul Wright; 86, Ron Case/Keystone; 92, Keystone-France/Gamma Keystone; 96–97, David Redfern/Redferns; 102–103, PYMCA/UIG; 104, Haynes Archive/Popperfoto; 106–107, Michael Ochs Archives; 109, Ron Case, 110–111, Terry Fincher/Express/Hulton Archive; 112, Keystone-France/Gamma-Rapho; 114–115, Philip McAllister/Moment Editorial; 116–117, Terence Spencer/The LIFE Images Collection; 119, Paul Popper/Popperfoto; 120, Popperfoto; 122–123, Bentley Archive/Popperfoto; 126–127, Universal/Corbis/VCG; 132–133, Daily Mirror/Mirrorpix; 134, Janette Beckman; 135, Paul Popper/Popperfoto; 136, Dan Kitwood; 141, James Whitmore/The LIFE Images Collection; 142–143, Daily Express/Hulton Archive; 144–145, Hulton-Deutsch Collection/CORBIS; 151, Daily Mirror/Mirrorpix; 156, SAM PANTHAKY/AFP; 164–165, Popperfoto; 167, Laura Lezza; 173, Slim Aarons; 198–199, INA FASSSBENDER/AFP; 210, Eric Lafforgue/Art In All Of Us/Corbis; 215, Joerg Mitter/Global-Newsroom; 216–217, Doug McKinlay; 220–221, Ed Wray; 222–223, Yvan Cohen/LighRocket

LIBRARY OF CONGRESS

Pages 18–19, Harris & Ewing Collection

MAGNUM PHOTOS

Pages 6–7, Ferdinando Scianna; 44–45, Bruno Barbey; 98–99, Chris Steele-Perkins; 161, Leonard Freed

MOTORBOOKS COLLECTION

Page 64, 157, 204–205

PATRICIA PICCININI

Pages 138–139: Nest, 2006. Fibreglass, auto paint, leather, steel, polycarbonate. 90 x 150 x 170cm. Courtesy of the Artist, and Tolarno, Roslyn Oxley9 and Hosfelt Galleries. Page 234: The Lovers, 2011. Fibreglass, auto paint, leather, scooter parts. 202 x 205 x 130 cm. Courtesy of the Artist, and Tolarno, Roslyn Oxley9 and Hosfelt Galleries

RICHARD PETTIFER, DOUBLEGOOD.CO.UK

Illustrations pages 66, 73, 194, 214

SHUTTERSTOCK

Page 4, Dax101; 5, Lenscap Photography; 56–57, ermess; 72–73, aon 168; 80–81, Hans Christiansson; 158–159, ermess; 219, ZDL

INDEX

POLICE NOTICE
NO
WAITING